Understar 192161

Series Editors
Christoph Meinel
Larry Leifer

For other titles published in this series, go to
http://www.springer.com/series/8802

Yukio Ohsawa • Yoko Nishihara

Innovators' Marketplace

Using Games to Activate and Train Innovators

 Springer

Yukio Ohsawa
The University of Tokyo
School of Engineering
Department of Systems Innovation
Tokyo
Japan
ohsawa@sys.t.u-tokyo.ac.jp

Yoko Nishihara
The University of Tokyo
School of Engineering
Department of Systems Innovation
Tokyo
Japan
nishihara@sys.t.u-tokyo.ac.jp

ISBN 978-3-642-25479-6   e-ISBN 978-3-642-25480-2
DOI 10.1007/978-3-642-25480-2
Springer Heidelberg Dordrecht London New York

Library of Congress Control Number: 2012931937

Printed on acid-free paper

Springer is part of Springer Science+Business Media (www.springer.com)

Foreword

The authors have been hunting diligently to develop insights into the causality of complex socio-technical systems, including: products, services, businesses, and enterprises at all scales. The Innovators' Marketplace is a structured activity that increases the probability of discovery, less by chance, more by design.

In this regard their earlier book, "Chance Discovery," offers a timely duality in the meaning and utility of the phrase. From one point-of-view it is all about how to discover a chance to innovate. In the alternative point-of-view, it is all about increasing the probability of a chance to discover. In fact they are pragmatic realists deeply committed to evidence based exploration, analytics in the face of un-measurable uncertainty and ambiguity. Their pragmatism is revealed in the requirement that one balance the two points-of-view, letting neither become a fixation, a rut, or worst of all, a dogma that would diminish our chance to innovate.

In my own laboratory, we have found a hunting metaphor is an effective means for communicating the importance of developing good hunting skills (you might call them gaming skills). With our unit of analysis focused on the hunting team we are at all times following the advice of Ohsawa and Nishihara to keep the interests, needs, and real life actions of all stake holders in view and in balance. It makes for a better team, a better game, and a better chance discovery opportunity in the Innovators' Marketplace.

I especially appreciate the author's highly integrative approach. Examples, cases, and literature citations are highly diversified. Their strategy helps assure me that the methods and results have broad applicability and impact potential.

The Innovators' Market Game has matured from a thought piece, through several development stages and validation experiments. Its maturity deserves your attention. In many situations, it will be the tool of choice for dealing with ambiguity. Never stop hunting. Deliver your discoveries to the market.

Stanford
Stanford University

Larry Leifer

Preface

In today's reality, it has become increasingly important to sense values of the events and details of everyday life. For example, a small earthquake may be the sign of a big quake in the future, and we should take careful note in order to prevent or reduce possible damage in advance. Another example is a claim by a picky customer who calls the customer relations section of a company and points out a serious problem in a product. In this case, the section manager should assume that a flood of similar claims may arise in the near future. Even if this assumption is too harsh, he should talk to product designers about the invention of a service or a new design of the product to reduce negative reactions from customers – and from potential customers, who may become loyal customers if they are satisfied with the company's products. In both examples, individuals have to plan a scenario, that is the series of future actions and events by estimating the value of an observed event with respect to the dynamics of the real world.

There are countless examples of events that have had a positive impact on the human lifestyle. When mobile phones first entered the market in the 1990s, they were used only by exceptionally rich individuals and business workers, but then the consumer base expanded to include high school students and finally diffused all over the social spectrum (and the world) as the shapes and functions of the phones evolved. The product designers took advantage of a rare event: exceptionally positive/negative consumer reaction to a new product every time it was produced. The designers used their understanding (or even misunderstanding) of the event to develop functions and designs to satisfy the new requirements, and the consumers reacted to the appearance of new products by creating new lifestyles. In other words, the combination of the cognitive processes of suppliers and demanders brought about the evolution of the market and of the technologies.

Since 2000, we have been organizing workshops and conference sessions on *chance discovery*. Chance discovery is defined in our community as the discovery **of** chance, rather than discovery **by** chance, as we will discuss in Chaps. 2 and 3. A "chance" here means a new event/situation that can be viewed as either an opportunity or a risk. The "discovery" of chances is of crucial importance because they may have a significant impact on human decision making. Desirable effects of opportunities should be actively promoted, while preventive measures should be taken in the case of discovered risks. In other words, the aim of chance discovery is to provide means for inventing or surviving the future rather than simply predicting the future.

We have developed chance discovery as a research area to figure out how to discover rare or novel events causing potentially significant outcomes. Although an event itself might not be significant, a chance can be linked to the emergence of significant scenarios – a series of actions and events in a coherent context – in the future. The context can be a constraint posed by the requirements of other people, or it can be an intention to achieve a given/created goal. Using computers to visualize relationships among events can enhance the ability of individuals to externalize potential scenarios, enabling them to discover chances and thus contribute to beneficial strides forward in business. We have achieved significant success in the detection of chance by applying our original technologies of data mining/visualization to natural/social events and human behaviors in the field of commerce.

Overall, our methods are based on one basic principle: computers are good at generatively simulating scenarios derivable from countable conditions, whereas humans are good at paying attention to the essential parts of the real world, i.e., the most interesting scenarios. In order to take advantage of both, our method of chance discovery follows a four-step spiral, which has since been used by individuals in the business, political, and scientific fields to improve innovation in their respective domains. This four-step spiral is shown below:

(1) Collect data from the real world that is explicitly or implicitly affected by an individual's sense of value.
(2) Analyze and visualize the collected data using computer(s).
(3) Verbally externalize, i.e., write/speak about, scenarios underlying the visualized structure of the relationships among events.
(4) Communicate with other individuals, who interpret the same visualization result from different viewpoints, to find the novel value of events at the cross-points of scenarios and to externalize one's own sense of value. Then, return to step (1).

For practical application to real businesses, we used (with creating if necessary) some or all of the following technologies to reinforce each step: artificial sensor devices such as RFID tags for step (1), computational data mining/visualization software for step (2), and Web-based thinking/communicating environments for improving the efficiency of steps (3) and (4).

We interviewed people who have applied our method to manufacturing, services, advertising, marketing, medicine, politics, education, and scientific studies. Our common understanding after these discussions is that ultimately, individuals need to be prepared with basic knowledge about the dynamism of the parts of the society relevant to themselves, and that organizations should have an atmosphere conducive to the never-ending spiral of steps (1)–(4). Also, users should not skip the preparatory phases that come in advance (i.e., before step (1)). In other words, our chance discovery method does not always work if it is not used properly.

Since 2005, we have been expanding chance discovery, which was originally focused on new events significant for human decision making, to include value sensing, particularly in the world of business. As discussed in more detail later in the introduction, the difference between chance discovery and value sensing is that the latter has the potential capacity to deal with a broader range of valuable events. Value sensing can cover events that are high frequency, low frequency, zero frequency (events that have never observed or captured in data), and even events that occur only in the imagination, whereas chance discovery is mainly focused on the values of low-frequency events stored in real-time data. This expansion enables us to obtain innovative ideas from both human minds that are thinking about personal affairs and computers that are dealing with observed events in a natural/social environment.

In this book, we introduce games we have developed to train and activate value sensing in both individuals and groups. We present case studies showing how our *Innovators' Market Game* (IMG) and *Analogy Game* (AG) make the spiral of value sensing easier to execute and more productive due to enhanced human ability. This process of improvement is called the Innovators' Marketplace. "Market" and "Marketplace" are used metaphorically to describe the interactions among users (players) who communicate with each other to create realistic ideas for business strategies. That is, some players invent ideas by combining pre-existing basic individual ideas, while others evaluate the value of those ideas before deciding whether or not to buy. This interaction is primarily activated in IMG, which, our 10 years of experience with chance discovery, has prompted us to propose it as a tool for aiding innovative thought and communication.

IMG enabled participants (whom we call *players*) to both direct and accelerate the process of innovation, which is our ultimate goal. We consider innovation not pure creativity but rather the creation of a product, service, or a system of products and services that will be viewed as of high-positive impact by consumers and potential customers/clients in the real market. We wanted players to not only invent a new idea but also evaluate ideas by considering the existing and potential requirements of consumers. IMG is a realization of this requirement, i.e., inventions and the evaluation of inventions, in the market of ideas. The Analogy Game (AG) is used for enhancing the process of Innovators' Marketplace by being combined with IMG. Here, the users basically play alone, arranging and rearranging words on a two-dimensional display so that new concepts common to multiple words can be externalized. This can be used either as a tool for externalizing hidden concepts underlying popular words (discussed in Chap. 5) or as the pre-process of the Innovators' Market Game (discussed in Chap. 9). Case studies of these games in actual use are presented in Chaps. 8 and 9. Note that we could only publish a few cases from among a large number of successful marketplace applications because practitioners seldom allowed us to reveal successful cases to the public.

After playing IMG, the players start to evaluate created ideas more seriously considering actual business situations and choose ideas that are more likely to succeed as products. In Chap. 10, we describe a Web-based environment we created for continuing the flow of innovative thought and communication. Players utilize this resource after completing IMG in order to continue improving obtained ideas.

We also compare the effects of IMG when used as a board game and when used in a Web-based environment. It will be shown that there are some aspects of innovative communication we can enhance, some on the table and some on the Web. Although the results for Web-IMG are not yet as encouraging as those for the board game version (face-to-face), experimental results have shown us where to direct our future work. They also highlighted the practical aspects of merging the face-to-face version with the computer-mediated one. More importantly, the novel model for interaction between the cognitive spirals of inventors and consumers provides us with a new way to discuss the processes of innovation in which individuals, products, and services connect the two spirals.

In concluding this preface, we wish the reader to understand why it is so important to play games. The Innovators' Marketplace is a marketplace of ideas, where various resources representing value – money, stocks, products, services, individuals, technologies, and knowledge – are exchanged. The voices of inventors, consumers, and investors are added to the flow of these resources to construct and destruct new ideas about products, services, and all manner of business scenarios. Such exchanges can sometimes involve serious conflicts, which may discourage participants because of the difficulty of surviving the hard times associated with the inventions, evaluations, and realizations of practical scenarios. What would you want the most in such a situation? If we were you, we would desire a joyful communication atmosphere in order to make our organization a sustainable system of innovation. The joyful air thanks to using games is a source of power that is generated by the Innovators' Marketplace and runs itself. The energy for enhancing, training, and reusing individual's thoughts and communications for innovation can be supplied by this self-productive, positive-feedback engine.

Tokyo   *Yukio Ohsawa*
                                                                                Yoko Nishihara

Acknowledgments

We thank Christoph Meinel and Larry Leifer for inviting us to write this book. The insights and strong will that led to this publication were the fruits of their encouragement. Both of these individuals are major contributors in the field of innovation, and we are in their debt. We also express our sincere thanks to Dr. Martin Steinert, acting Assistant Professor and Deputy Director of the Center for Design Research at Stanford University, who connected the authors who were originally communicating with Prof. Larry Leifer in Stanford University, also to Prof. Christoph Meinel at Hasso Plattner Institute in Potsdam, DE. Dr. Steinert worked as the bridging node, whose importance should be understandable for readers who read up this book.

Contents

List of Figures

List of Tables

Chapter 1
Introduction: Innovation as a Serious Entertainment

1.1 What is an Innovation?

One century has passed since Joseph Schumpeter defined the concept of *innovation* as "the introduction of new goods, new methods of production, the opening of new markets, the conquest of new sources of supply, and the carrying out of a new organization of any industry" (Schumpeter 1912/1934). This definition can sometimes be confusing because "goods" and "methods" seem to be very different things, and a "market" is a mixture of these properties plus other factors such as money and individuals (suppliers, consumers, and stakeholders). However, after much thought, we have concluded that this definition is suitable for expressing what we need in this century of changes to hardware, software, networks, natural/social resources, the environment, information, and even human modes of thought. We need a new way of looking at this flood: a way of creating something that has a value beyond that of the most attractive existing commodities, thereby developing a new direction for the growth of the market.

Since the work of Schumpeter, there have been other definitions of innovation proposed from various domains, including sociology, engineering, and business:

- "A change that creates a new dimension of performance." (Peter Drucker, management consultant and social ecologist)
- "A new element introduced in the network which changes, even if momentarily, the costs of transactions between at least two actors, elements or nodes, in the network." (Regis Cabral, technology management scientist)
- "The three stages in the process of innovation: invention, translation, and commercialization." (Merrifield 1986)
- "An invention is an idea, a sketch or model for a new or improved device, product, process, or system .... An innovation in the economic sense is accompanied with the first commercial transaction involving the new product, process, system or device, although the word is used to describe the whole process." (Freeman 1982)
- "The ability to deliver new value to a customer." (Campos 1999)

Y. Ohsawa and Y. Nishihara, *Innovators' Marketplace*, Understanding Innovation,
DOI 10.1007/978-3-642-25480-2_1, © Springer-Verlag Berlin Heidelberg 2012

- "The way of transforming the resources of an enterprise through the creativity of people into new resources and wealth." (Schumann 2009)

The idea common to all these definitions is that innovation is a form of *potentially desired creativity*, not just an isolated creative activity. That is, an innovation must promise an appealing new value. We know that the product obtained from an innovation should be accepted by a large number of people, but very few people can actually think of such a product in advance: for example, the World Wide Web would not be called an innovation today if everybody was already talking about it back in the 1980s. This dilemma can make people feel that innovation is something miraculous done by a "special" type of individual, not an ordinary person such as we would daily meet in real life. However, if we look around at the commodities we use on a daily basis, it is obvious that there is a large number of people who have created these commodities, and an even larger number who have launched them in the market. In the next section, we take a look at some of the creators of everyday commodities.

1.2 Who Innovates?

Here, we discuss a couple of historical cases of innovation that demonstrate the complexity of the social interaction between stakeholders and technologies.

1.2.1 Edison Versus Swan: Who Invented the Light Bulb?

In a classroom setting, if students are asked "Who created the light bulb?" the first answer tends to be "Thomas Edison." However, this is not correct. Although Edison is extremely famous as an inventor, the credit for the light bulb should rather go to Joseph Swan, who led to the emergence of this very popular item that today is prevalent all over the world.

Joseph Swan was born in 1828 in Sunderland, England. He worked for a pharmacy and it was there he learned the basic technologies for producing medicine. He later became the vice president of a pharmacy in Newcastle, "Mawson, Swan, & Morgan Co. Ltd," which stayed in business until 1973. As early as 1848, he was experimenting with the concept of the light bulb. His basic method was to implement a carbonized filament made of paper in a vacuumed glass ball. By 1860, he had successfully lit a prototype light bulb, which was patented in the UK. However, this invention was not successfully commercialized because of the incompleteness of the vacuum and the insufficient amount of power supplied. The most critical issue was not being able to sustain the light.

Fifteen years later, Swan had improved the vacuuming technology and invented a long-expectancy carbon filament. He then turned his attention to solving the

Fig. 1.1 Light bulbs of
Edison (*left*) and Swan
(*right*): figure from
Wikimedia Commons

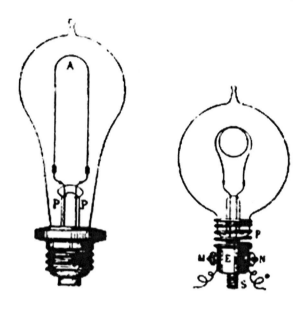

remaining problem. In 1878, he discovered that if a small amount of oxygen was
in the glass ball, the filament continued to glow for 40 h. Swan obtained a patent,
but the power supply was not stable due to the low resistance of the filament. His
house in Gateshead became the first in the world to use a light bulb. In 1881, Swan
established the Swan Electric Light Company.

In 1879 – some years after Swan's success – Edison created a light bulb using
his own original filament. Edison's new light bulb had a straight filament, and its
light could be sustained for nearly as long as Swan's (Fig. 1.1). Then in 1880, he
improved the filament by using Japanese bamboo as the material and achieved an
impressive sustainability of light: as long as 2,450 h. Edison and Swan integrated
their respective companies into the Edison and Swan United Electric Company.
Thereafter, Swan invented a filament using a new method for processing cellulose
that finally came into commercial use due to the availability of the material and
the durability achieved by the invention. Swan and Edison were engaged in a close
race with their filament inventions, as well as in legal disputes regarding light bulb
patents, so it is difficult to judge who really invented the commercialized light bulb
used today.

However, today, most of us believe that Edison invented the light bulb because of
his sophisticated business acumen. Three million people were using his light bulb
20 years after he established his new company, and 25% of houses in the US had
adopted it within the next 20 years. There are some uncertain hypotheses explaining
Edison's success, but what is certain is that he invented major accessories (socket,
safety fuse, power meter, switchboard, etc.) to ensure safe lighting and circulation of
electricity throughout towns. This apparently meets all the definitions of innovation
we mentioned in the previous section.

This example shows that innovation comes from the process of creating inventions using established knowledge (a vacuumed light bulb with carbonized filament) and novel concepts (e.g., bamboo filament and accessories) combined with competition and communication among inventors. With changes to the human lifestyle due to the circulation of electricity, people accepted later technologies invented by Edison himself and his successors to satisfy the new demands that had been created. This shows that innovation is also a result of the interaction between inventors and consumers. The answer to the question "Who invented the light bulb?" is not easy, but if we alter the question to "Who innovated human society with the light bulb?" we could answer, "All inventors and all consumers."

1.2.2 Microsoft Versus Apple Versus Google

It was when the first author (Ohsawa) attended the Conference of World Wide Web in Brisbane in 1998, that an interesting paper attracted him, titled "The Anatomy of a Large-scale Hypertextual Web-search Engine" and co-authored by Sergey Brin and Larry Page (Brin and Page 1998). This paper concluded with a vision for the future: "Our immediate goals are to improve search efficiency and to scale to approximately 100 million Web pages. Some simple improvements to efficiency include query caching, smart disk allocation, and sub-indices." Today, we know that Google, which was founded by the co-authors of this paper, has indexed as many as 40 billion pages, and a spin-off search engine called Cuil was able to index 120 billion pages (although it has since been shut down). We all know that Google expanded to include much more than query caching, including Google Earth with its street view function, Google TV, and much more to reach far beyond the boundary of information retrieval on the Web.

Ten years ago, around 2000, Microsoft was clearly the leader in the computer software field. Some people said Microsoft was like Sony, which had created a brand image through original products. However, this is incorrect if we take a closer look at what Macintosh was doing around 1990. Macintosh's GUI, which was produced by Apple, seemed almost magical when it first appeared. Before then, we had only the command-prompt interface of Microsoft DOS when we Japanese students were using the PC9800 series produced by NEC in Japan, and had to manually type commands when we wanted the PC to do anything. Microsoft Windows 3.x appeared just after this period of time – from 1991 – and was not as easy to use or as visually attractive as the Macintosh. We could not at all feel any sign of the future prevalence of Microsoft's GUI-based OS. After that, a lot more "magic" appeared, such as the Web browser Mosaic, followed by Netscape, which was then overwhelmed by Microsoft's Internet Explorer. We did not yet have Microsoft Excel, and Lotus-123 by Lotus Development was the strongest data table management software available. All these software categories were eventually overwhelmed by Microsoft, and ordinary people adapted to this trend and installed MS products on their PCs.

Fig. 1.2 iPhone and iPad: who invented the latter?

Considering this short history, it is clear that the PC software market was not originally dominated by Microsoft: Apple, Netscape, and others should be acknowledged as well. However, we can say that Microsoft cultivated this field by integrating tools to organize a system of services for PC users. For example, users naturally assume that data processed on Excel can be shared on the Web by using a browser, and that whatever OS we use should be able to support both Excel and the browser and also other sophisticated packaged software. Microsoft's strategy of selling PowerPoint, Excel, Word, etc., in one package was a direct result of their analysis of consumer habits. In other words, Microsoft invented the idea of improving existing items by combining them via interactions with the market.

Decades passed, and currently Apple seems to be doing well in the race with Microsoft. Apple continued to develop its own central software (OS), application platforms, and hardware throughout the difficult period, which enabled it to invent an overall system of information processing for ordinary users rather than focusing on one or a few components. That is, Apple developed popular items such as the iPod, iPhone, and iPad, which are not PC accessories but rather components of daily life endowed with rich information. Apple not only survived but also evolved because it was able to create a new type of human lifestyle. An interesting rumor is that Alan Kay, the father of the PC, hinted to Steven Jobs that he should enlarge the display of the iPhone, which led Jobs to invent the iPad (Fig. 1.2). If this is true, we can conclude that Apple obtained the basic idea for the iPad by combining the basic ideas of the smartphone and the PC.

Next, let us shift our focus to Google, which has progressed far beyond the "future work" mentioned by Brin and Page in 1998. Because its fundamental business model is to increase the number of advertisements on the www.google.com page, they do not aim to sell their original OS. This may be why they provide users and hardware manufacturers (of both PCs and smartphones) with free OSs. This fundamental strategy has accelerated the diffusion of the Google OS. In other words, Google is evolving due to both its starting point as an inventor of the search engine and its understanding of the growing industry of smartphones as its new market. As a result, it is difficult to picture the Microsoft OS beating out the Google OS, Android. At present, Apple and Google are clearly the two leaders in this market.

These two leaders are extending their reach to the television market. Apple TV is hardware that is basically an ordinary TV set on which content other than TV programs can be viewed. This content includes movies supplied by Paramount Pictures, Walt Disney Studio, Universal Pictures, 20th Century Fox, etc., YouTube videos and music, pictures from MobileMe, etc., and music streamed from a PC. With Google TV, users can enjoy Web browsing, Twitter, videos streamed from YouTube, Blue Ray, and applications downloaded from the Android Market. The low price of these TV systems is appealing to potential users, most of whom are waiting for a good opportunity to swap their current TV for an Apple or Google version. Smartphones with Android (Google OS) and the Apple OS can be used as the remote controller for Google TV and Apple TV. The consumer demand for low-cost replacement TV sets has been taken into account in these two companies' marketing strategies.

These three firms – Microsoft, Apple, and Google – have combined new concepts, some of which were borrowed from others, as a response to market demands, resulting in periods of dramatically increased business. Although the number of combinations they are working with has increased drastically since the era of Edison, the fundamental principle for innovation is essentially the same.

1.3 Innovation as a Serious Entertainment

1.3.1 Consumers Who Contribute to Innovation

> Innovation does not relate just to a new product that would come into the marketplace. Innovation can occur in processes and approaches to the marketplace. (David Schmittlein, Professor of Marketing at MIT Sloan School)

As we discussed in the previous section, the real innovation behind a strong social impact is not a single "creative" thought or action by which the economy is transformed into a new state. Rather, innovation is caused by the process of interaction among stakeholders in the market. If this were not so, the combination of industrial resources, such as existing technologies and knowledge of business, could not be continued until the fruit of a desirable product or service came to

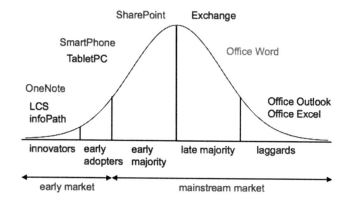

Fig. 1.3 The stakeholders of innovation and diffusion

light. It is noteworthy that the word "innovation" was originally presented not as a synonym of creation but as the process of activities leading up to the introduction of new goods or methods and thereby opening new markets in all domains of business: manufacturing, logistics, services, etc. This can be traced back to the age of Henry Ford, who established a company and introduced conveyer belt systems as a part of the business process, and of Edison, who changed the lifestyles of town dwellers with his promotion of electric power. Knowledge and technologies born from innovation should be regarded as entities processed in a way that is more complex than products that are made in factories. Not only workers employed in the factory but also consumers and customers should join the process – not in a factory surrounded by walls, but out in the world where potential customers may desire new technologies without even being aware of their desires. Half a century after Shumpeter defined innovation, Rogers (Rogers 1962) pointed out that some leading consumers play the role of *innovators*. Even a very good idea cannot become an innovation without these consumers on the side of innovation. Consumers called *early adopters* are the first to embrace a new product or service, and they are then followed by the *majority*. The *laggard* might or might not follow, which signals the final state of diffusion (Fig. 1.3). To think of this in visual terms, the process of diffusion looks like one of Henry Ford's conveyer belts.

However, the existence of a *chasm*, which is the gap between the different types of consumers (such as between the early adopters and the early majority) implies that there is a contextual gap between consumer communities (Moore 1991). A strategy to bridge the chasm, according to Moore, is to detect and focus on the most promising segment of consumers in the early majority and then to integrate knowledge of multiple business domains to compose a value for people in the majority via this detected segment. Rogers, however, explicitly rejects Moore's chasm theory in his revised book (Rogers 2003) due to his belief that the innovation value, if evaluated properly, will be diffused without discontinuity at what Moore called the chasm. In other words, Moore proposed that the value of a well-designed use scenario for an invented product/service, if evaluated in a suitable context, would not be rejected on the way to diffusion due to lukewarm interest or a late response on behalf of the consumer.

In our opinion, these two theories are not mutually exclusive, because segmenting consumers and choosing one segment, as Moore suggested, is a way of focusing on a suitable context, as Rogers implied, in which we can properly evaluate a usage scenario. We should also point out that identifying a user's tentative situation rather than his/her personality can be a promising way to focus on a suitable context, which has been presented as "situation-based marketing" (Washida et al. 2004). For example, we can guide traveling users of a mobile phone to a suitable restaurant by detecting their location with GPS, and we can analyze users' emotional states by going over e-mail logs and data on heartbeats. Essentially, we can generalize the two approaches for moving beyond the hurdle in the diffusion of innovation by the following two steps:

(1) Identify a suitable context and a scenario based on that context in which the value of an invented product/service will be sensed by consumers.
(2) Circulate a message that externalizes the (context, scenario) set in the form of a story broadcast to consumers who live in the corresponding context or of a product/service provided in a place and at a time matching the context.

The requirements for moving beyond the hurdle can be reduced to the question "How can we carry out steps (1) and (2)?" The former can be regarded as a problem of *scenariozation*, while the latter is of *realization*. Who can solve these problems, and how?

Eric von Hippel's recent book *Democratizing Innovation* gives us a good hint for answering this question: there are leading consumers who not only use and diffuse but also invent ideas and technologies to improve/expand a product to fit their own contexts. Such lead users may function as a link between innovators and early adopters and can play the role of change-agent (Rogers 2003). For example, some technologies for producing mountain bikes have been invented by leading users who thought up new designs to solve daily problems they encountered when using the bikes themselves. Product developers/designers in manufacturing firms had the opportunity to contact these lead users and converse with them, and ultimately they obtained valuable insight into how to create more useful products. Here, the interaction between innovators in the market (i.e., lead consumers) and innovators in the industry became the key to opening the minds of stakeholders on each side. Thus, "innovators" really means all people contributing to innovation, who are all stakeholders of services and products to be created in the market, taking part in communication to externalize and satisfy the potential desires of consumers.

In order to achieve innovation, or to sustain innovation in the face of growing competition, many ask the question "How can we find leading users, or whoever else might continuously contribute to this innovation?" von Hippel introduced a method of networking to detect leading users in which the investigator traces the route of an idea to find the actual person who invented the useful technology. Tracing the paths in the network of human relations is often effective for mining and inviting

Fig. 1.4 Cyclists with various types of bicycles meet on holiday, where they naturally start talking. A cyclist who usually commutes on paved roads may learn how an MTB is just as comfortable for off-road use as for recreation, and vice versa. A new bike combining a road racer and an MTB may be invented in the near future from such a community

latent contributors to the innovation process. An example of this is shown in Fig. 1.4: mountain bikers organize communities via the natural process of forming human relationships in daily life and start talking about new ideas for more comfortable rides. In the next section, we describe a case in which another type of stakeholder, called mediators, worked to create a meeting between expected contributors and inventors.

1.3.2 Other Stakeholders of Innovation: Edison Revisited

In the garden of Iwashimizu Hachiman shrine in Kyoto, Japan, we find a monument "To the Memory of Thomas Alva Edison" (Fig. 1.5). The back of this monument describes his invention of the light bulb and his relationship with Japan (translated from Japanese): "Thomas Alva Edison, from the United States of America, had a great talent and an outstanding vitality. He achieved a huge number of inventions, one of which, the light bulb, became one of the most remarkable contributions to human life in world history. He extensively studied various carbonized fibers and ultimately chose to use bamboo as the fiber material for light bulbs. In 2540 of the Japanese Imperial era (corresponding to year 1880 of the Gregorian calendar), Edison sent an assistant to Japan. The governor of Kyoto prefecture at that time, Uemura Masanao, recommended that this assistant use the bamboo from this shrine, which Edison then used to finally create a long-lasting light...." We can skip the remainder of this quotation, because the preceding excerpt should be enough to illustrate how the people in Japan welcomed the visit of Edison's assistant and are proud of their role in this part of history.

Fig. 1.5 Edison's monument in Iwashimizu Hachiman, Kyoto

Let us now look at Uemura Masanao, the governor of Kyoto at the time of Edison's innovation. Uemura is known to have been of a politician with a strong attitude: e.g., he rejected the movement of some powerful merchandisers from Kyoto to other cities in Japan, and he did not change this decision even after the Japanese court ordered him to do so. It might seem a little surprising to hear that such a man not only welcomed Moore, Edison's assistant, but also recommended that he visit the Iwashimizu Hachiman shrine, which is still famous in the present century for its rich, high-quality bamboo. Why did Uemura accept him with such grace and kindness?

We do know that Uemura was interested in science and technology from foreign countries. He invited Fukuzawa Yukichi, who had previously established a multidisciplinary school of medical science, economics, law, etc., in Tokyo (Keio Gijuku, which later became Keio University) using knowledge he had imported from outside of Japan, to Kyoto to build a branch of Keio Gijuku. This strong interest of Uemura in science may be one reason for his acceptance of Moore.

However, it is not yet fully clear why he was kindly disposed toward Moore. It is true that Edison had a strong relationship with Japan: indeed, the founder of Nippon Electricity Corporation (NEC) once worked for the Edison Machine Work company. However, this was after Edison sent Moore to Japan in 1880. There is another link between Edison and Uemura that we need to consider.

By that period of time, Edison had invested $100,000 to send 20 scientists all over the world in order to collect as many as 6,000 species of plant fiber. On the way, they studied more than 1,000 kinds of bamboo from various Asian countries and performed experiments to evaluate the durability of lighting using

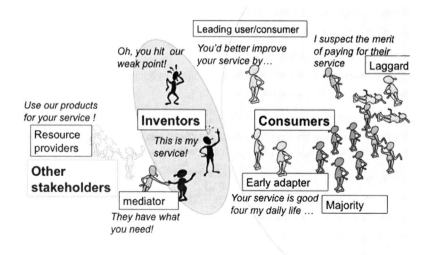

Fig. 1.6 The innovator marketplace. Here, "innovator" means all people contributing to an innovation, all of whom are stakeholders of the market and communicate with each other to externalize and satisfy potential desires

bamboo filaments. Among those countries, Japan was noteworthy in that it was in the midst of the Meiji Restoration. Political power had shifted from the Shogun to the Emperor, and the importation of culture and technologies from outside of Japan became a high-priority mission of the new government.

Conditions were perfect for Japan to accept Edison, who was already famous as a technology leader for having invented the sound recorder. However, it would have been next to impossible for a foreigner to harvest bamboo from the garden of the Imperial House of Japan's second most important shrine. It is not an unreasonable guess that someone in the Japanese government headquarters contacted either Edison or Moore and actually invited Edison's team to use the bamboo at Iwashimizu Hachiman for their research. The governor of Kyoto would certainly not have had access to this kind of authority. In fact, Moore met prime minister Ito Hirobumi before he met Uemura: the prime minister acted as mediator, and it was he who arranged the meeting between Moore and Uemura.

Here, we should briefly note that there was a party of politicians born in the province of Choshu who came to lead the Japanese government just after the Meiji Restoration. Ito and Uemura were among these politicians, and because there were rival political parties, it is safe to assume that the Choshu group wanted something with a strong impact to attract the national interest of the Japanese people. Essentially, there were three primary factors in place before Edison and Moore were able to reach the bamboo at Iwashimizu:

(1) Edison and Moore's requirement of a suitable material for producing a high-durability filament.
(2) The political constraint on Japan, which may have disturbed Edison and Moore from accessing the bamboo.
(3) The requirement of a political group in Japan to have a close relationship with technological leaders outside of Japan.

As a by-product, Kyoto would reap economic benefits by exporting native bamboo. In the context of the interaction between inventors and consumers we touched on in the previous section, Edison and Moore were inventors while the politicians, although not contributing to the innovation from the standpoint of consumers, nevertheless played a significant role as the mediator of relationships between inventors and the suppliers of the material.

So far, we have described how innovation is essentially the fruit of teamwork in the form of interaction between stakeholders (including industrial inventors), sensitive and communicative consumers, consumers who invent, and even those who are linked to these people via politics rather than commerce. Figure 1.6 shows a simplified, abstract illustration of the world of stakeholders (an actual market, of course, is much more complex).

1.3.3   Serious Entertainment

As we will show in Chap. 6, stakeholders should not only ensure a friendly communication atmosphere but also motivate the participants of the market to question and to constructively criticize each other's ideas. This might not be the most pleasant situation for the inventors, especially if the contextual discrepancy among stakeholders is large. In addition, if communications become too heated, the whole interaction may have to be terminated. In this sense, we recommend that stakeholders other than inventors, who will not hesitate to negate the value of an invention, make their comments with carefully reflecting the context of the users of the invented products that the inventor proposes. For example, if the Japanese politicians had refused to export bamboo to Edison's company due to the religious importance of the shrine's garden, Edison might have been unable to continue his business relationship with Japan because the contextual discrepancy between the technology for the new human lifestyle and the traditional religion would be beyond the reach of negotiation.

However, this is not a realistic request of most players. We mentioned above that players (stakeholders of different contexts) should consider each other's contexts carefully to ensure that even negative comments are delivered in an atmosphere that remains positive. However, put yourself in Edison's shoes: would you have had enough sensitivity to understand the religious background of Japan when you probably had many other countries to visit? Maybe not. This highlights the need for a method of communication that enables all players, even stakeholders coming from very different contexts, to comfortably exchange inventions and opinions that may involve serious disputes or severe criticisms.

The Innovators' Marketplace (IM) we present in this book is a simple but powerful method for creating a system of innovation that includes combinatorial and analogical thoughts, the involvement of stakeholders in the market, and interdisciplinary communication and interaction in an enjoynable atmosphere. This atmosphere, which is created by the games integrated in the process, motivates participants to look beyond resistance to negativity or criticism. In this book, we demonstrate Schumpeter's point that an interdisciplinary combination of business actors and resources, possibly with the appearance of new actors, triggers innovation. We have added new participants, including consumers and even stock investors, who play from the viewpoint of someone indirectly involved in the market via transactions related to stocks.

In this introduction, we described a few examples of past innovations in which it was not clear who the real inventor was, as well as the importance of having stakeholders meet and maintain competition and interaction within the market. Sometimes, the inventor of an original technology gets overtaken by others who rethink the technology and diffuse an altered product, thereby emerging as the "winner." We regard such a transformation, which often occurs in tandem with other concepts, as a typical pattern of an innovation. The combination of existing technologies and ideas creates a value that goes beyond the sheer sum. Throughout this book, we postulate that the combination and cross-disciplinary transplantation of existing methods/resources of a given business to new problems via analogical thought and communication are the basic engines of innovation.

Our overall approach is twofold. First, develop a method to elevate the potential of innovations created by individuals in a group. They will become aware of their own positions as stakeholders in the market. Second, provide a communication environment for stakeholders in the market in which they can discuss future technologies and business so that they will also start thinking and talking about who the leading users (consumers) are in the market and where the best segment of the majority is. The games presented in this book, and the process that includes these games, are dedicated to this approach.

As discussed here, we emphasize there are people contributing to innovation on both the provider-side and the consumer-sides, and also in other groups of stakeholders. We all regard these people as innovators: The name Innovators' Marketplace we have given to the methodology presented in this book reflects this essential concept.

References

Brin S, Page L (1998) The anatomy of a large-scale hypertextual web search engine. In: Seventh international world-wide web conference (WWW 1998), Brisbane, 1998
Campos J (1999) A message in an exchange on definitions of innovation. http://www.innovation.cc/discussion-papers/definition.htm

Freeman C (1982) The economics of industrial innovation, 2nd edn. Frances Pinter, London

Merrifield BD (1986) Forces of change affecting high technology industries. A speech by U.S. assistant secretary of commerce

Moore GA (1991) Crossing the chasm: marketing and selling technology products to mainstream customers. Harper Business, New York

Rogers EM (1962) Diffusion of innovations, 1st edn. Free Press, Glencoe

Rogers EM (2003) Diffusion of innovations, 5th edn. Free Press, New York

Schumann P (2009) Building an innovative organization. Read on-line, ONREAD.COM, http://www.onread.com/reader/1043137/

Schumpeter JA (1912/1934) Theorie der wirtschaftlichen Entwicklung. Leipzig: Duncker and Humblot. English translation published in 1934 as The theory of economic development. Harvard University Press, Cambridge

WashidaY, Bjorn M, Kruse E (2004) Analysis of diffusion patterns of knowledge and new technology among Japanese early adopters: an ethnological study of product penetrations. In: Proceedings of IAMOT 2004 (International Association for Management of Technology 2004), #610 (CD-ROM), Washington D.C., US

Chapter 2
Chance Discovery as Value Sensing for Innovation

2.1 Modes of Intelligence and Emotion

As discussed in the previous chapter, we require participants in the market to understand other stakeholders' contexts and values in the market and to sustain interactions in order to realize their innovations. In other words, communication based on "cognitive empathy" is desired. As in the reference (Thompson 2001), cognitive empathy is not a disembodied and affectless knowing of the other, but rather the feeling of being led by another's experiences. Here, feeling means the integrated sense of bodily sensation and the emotional feeling of values.

The developmental psychologist Margaret Donaldson wrote that the essence of emotions is the feeling of value, and that human beings experience emotion only in regard to things in concern (Donaldson 1992). It is meaningful to borrow Thompson's understanding about Donaldson's theory, for interpreting innovation from the aspect of emotion and intelligence. She has shown that humans have as much potential for emotional development as for intellectual development, although the balance of the two may vary with social and cultural states. Donaldson modeled the development of the human mind on map with four main "modes of mind," each with four components: perception, action, thought, and emotion.

Each of the four modes is defined by its own "locus of concern." These include: (1) *the Point Mode*, of which the locus of concern is the present moment, "here and now" (available to young infants under 8 months); (2) *the Line Mode*, which appears at 8–10 months, of which the locus of concern is "there and then," expanded to include certain times in the personal past and personal future; (3) *the Construct Mode*, of which the locus of concern is "somewhere/sometime" (no specific place or time), emerging around the age of three; and (4) *the Transcendent Mode*, of which the locus of concern is "nowhere" (i.e., not in real space or time but in the spiritual world, which is beyond the imagination of the future world), which emerges around the age of nine.

Y. Ohsawa and Y. Nishihara, *Innovators' Marketplace*, Understanding Innovation, DOI 10.1007/978-3-642-25480-2_2, © Springer-Verlag Berlin Heidelberg 2012

Regarding the line mode, Donaldson wrote that the infant has a sort of "rolling" sense, i.e., the movement from the immediate past to the immediate present and to the immediate future. This mode enables the baby to oneself in relation to a remembered past and a possible future.

In the construct mode (3), one moves away from concrete personal events. Donaldson wrote that the mind will here begin to concern itself with a locus conceived as just somewhere/sometime, or anywhere/anytime, without fixating on a certain place or time. Thus, in this third mode, individuals are no longer restricted to a consideration of events that concretely exist in their own or colleague's experience. Individuals start to become actively and consciously concerned about the general nature of things. The mental context of humans here depends on their interaction with the environment involving deliberate constructive acts of imagination, rather than just passive perceptions or memories of events that occurred and have been perceived in the past. In some part of the construct mode, thought without emotion predominates over emotion. This is called the intellectual construct mode, where one is concerned about the nature of impersonal phenomena in space and time. As a result, humans can think of events and a series of events that they have never experienced: that is, they imagine scenarios that may have occurred in some past or may occur in some future.

Next, one moves from the intellectual construct mode to the transcendent mode, where the locus of concern is no longer bound to space and time. The feeling is not temporally or specially constrained. At this transcendent point, individuals are concerned with patterns of all kinds of relations into which things can enter. We can, for example, imagine a desirable mood in living without fixing the temporal order of events in a new life or space, develop faith in a religion, and understand others' concepts and abstract desires for comfortable living. Our sense of transcendent values may come in here, so the invariant values of love, peace, etc. can take place regardless of time and space. Donaldson asserts that there is a mode for emotions that develops in tandem with the intellectual modes above. This is called a *value-sensing mode*, with the proviso that the values in question must transcend personal concerns.

2.1.1 The Value-Sensing Modes

As Donaldson wrote and Thompson discussed, there are two value-sensing modes: the value-sensing construct mode and the value-sensing transcendent mode. These modes can be understood by linking them to the construct and transcendent modes above and introducing a new dimension of transpersonal relations to time and space. In the value-sensing construct mode, the main component of experience is an awareness of transpersonal importance that depends on the support of the imagination to identify the desires and feelings of others. In the value-sensing transcendent mode, self-transcending values can be experienced and responded to by properties that are beyond the imagination.

Donaldson says evidences of these modes in human thought can be found in the wisdom traditions that initiated religions, such as contemplative Christian mysticism, Buddhism, etc. For example, when St. John explained "how to reach divine union quickly," he distinguished between meditation, focusing on an image (such as a beautiful light), and contemplation, emptying oneself of all images so as to attain a receptive awareness of "divine union." Contemplation thus belongs to the value-sensing transcendent mode, where the locus of concern is not in space or time but something conceived as infinite and eternal and also as a non-measurable value. The value-sensing construct mode is more limited in its perception of value, since the "divine" surpasses anything we can imagine.

Although these studies are about infant development and not business people, the process of the development of intelligence and emotion is meaningful when discussing the co-elevation of the ability to objectively understand real events and the sense to subjectively expect values in the future. Under the assumption that the former corresponds to intellectual development while the latter at least partially corresponds to emotional development, we can conclude that objectivity and subjectivity both develop in accordance with an individual's interaction with the real-world environment.

When discussing innovation, we should take into account the discovery of values that underlies the market and that can be recognized by the innovator. Trends related to products and services existing in real space and real time should be grasped intelligently, and the emotional desires of potential consumers in the market, which have not been seen or imagined yet, should also be grasped thus. In this book, we do not discuss the highest level of value-sensing (the value-sensing transcendent mode) but rather focus on methods for elevating human ability corresponding to the value-sensing construct mode. However, if we regard religious or eco-centric lifestyles as forms of the transcendent mode and the different events in life, such as buying eco-oriented products to protect the environment, as the construct mode, it seems clear that Donaldson's modes should co-elevate that is, work at the same time with mutual reinforcement. Thus, we position our innovation-aid method as a method for cultivating and activating the human sense of values.

2.1.2 Compassion and Empathy

Let us return to learning from Thomson (2001). As he wrote, the progression of value-sensing modes leads to an acquisition i.e., an embedding of the egocentric sense of self. This acquisition is intuitively called "compassion" which is the super-concept of the human capacity for empathy. Compassion is regarded as a kind of value sensing that emerges as a result of inward meditation and also guides the progression of value-sensing modes.

Empathy precedes compassion and is a pre-requisite for compassion. When we feel empathy for someone, we are picking up emotional information about them and their situation. Collecting information about another's feelings allows us to get to know them better. As we get to know others on an emotional level, we are likely to see similarities between our own feelings and theirs, and between our basic emotional desires and theirs. When we realize that some of these basic emotional desires are similar to our own, we are better able to relate to others and to empathize with them. This point will play a role in later chapters of this book, in that emotional communication may enable players feel similarity to others, so that they can analogically create solutions to forthcoming problems.

Compassion can be defined as a combination of empathy and understanding. Greater empathy gives us more information for understanding things and people linked to ourselves. A higher level of emotion and intelligence creates a greater capacity for such understanding. Higher emotional sensitivity and awareness leads to higher levels of empathy, which leads to higher levels of understanding and then higher levels of compassion. As a result, we start to feel and understand how others feel. This dimension of emotion enables inventors and consumers deepen mutual understanding in Innovators Marketplace as in later chapters, via communication rich in emotion and intelligence.

In abstract terms, we can say that empathy should be established first, and then individuals can relate and co-elevate their values by exchanging emotional modes with each other, thereby reaching compassion. With this interaction and the deepened relationships among individuals, both emotional (subjective desire and feeling of connection with others) and intellectual (objective analysis and planning) modes are developed. Although Donaldson focused on the development of the minds of children, we feel we can extend her ideas to the training of grown adults because, even 30 years after we have graduated from schools, we daily experience new feelings that create new instances of empathy, compassion, and mutual understanding with people we have never created intimate relationships with in the past.

In the introduction of his paper, Thompson argues that we need the next step for new insights into human society (enlightenment in his words): He says we need to pursue a "science of interbeing" that integrates the methods of cognitive science, phenomenology, and the contemplative and meditative psychologies of the world's wisdom traditions. One of the essential aspects of this new progress is, according to him, the development of experimental techniques to assess the effect of value-sensing training, such as meditations on the equality of self and others and the mental putting of oneself in another's shoes.

It should be clear to the reader why we spent so much time discussing developmental education, which on the surface might seem irrelevant to innovation. Our point is that innovation is not the mere creation of something new but rather a combination of strategies and actions to join the emergence of a value-co-creative society, which amounts to a discontinuous development of the market. Thus, it is meaningful to extend the concept of intellectual and emotional development to the development of senses for creating business strategies based on experiences and new talents acquired in and going beyond experiences in the real world. The "value" here can be viewed as a relation to the social environment, which business workers and customers create from their interaction via products and services, in order to redesign the market sustainably.

2.2 Sensemaking Approach as a Basis of Qualitative Scenario Mining

For discussing information- and organization-scientific basis of our methods for innovation, we can also borrow concepts from studies on Sensemaking, meaning the process by which people give meaning to experiences (http://en.wikipedia.org/wiki/Sensemaking). It is a collaborative process of creating shared awareness and understanding of events via the collection of different individuals' perspectives and interests. Sensemaking has been discussed in organizational studies (Weick 1979) and in the field of information science (Dervin 1983).

In organizational studies, the concept of sensemaking has been used to express cognitive activities in general terms in order to focus on meaningful situations that have been experienced. In contrast, in information sciences as on the Web site created by Dervin (http://communication.sbs.ohio-state.edu/sense-making/), Sense-Making (capitalized) refers to the methodology, whereas sense-making (not capitalized) refers to the phenomena of making sense.

For the decisions and actions of organizations in uncertain or ambiguous situations, a central concept of sensemaking is *identification*, a process in which people interpret how they came into their current context by looking at a scenario in their past using methods of chance discovery (discussed later) and at a possible event in the future (Weick et al. 2005). Retrospection has been encouraged to aid with this identification process. The manner of retrospection, as well as the time it is focused on, affects what people notice (Dunford and Jones 2000). Then, people re-enact: i.e., they express the environments they face in dialogues and narratives (Watson 1998). As they speak and create narrative accounts, they understand what they themselves are thinking, organize their experiences, and are then able to control and predict events (Isabella 1990). In literature related to the cognitive sciences, retrospection and enactment are relevant to metacognition (Brown 1987;Flavell 1987;Cohen et al. 1996;Suwa 2008). We discuss metacognition in more detail in Chap. 4, as it plays an important role in the technical process of the Innovators' Marketplace.

An important point about sensemaking in organization is that it is a social activity. Plausible stories are preserved and shared among members of a group, communicating for their decision (Watson 1995). This social interaction is continued as individuals shape and react to the environments they face. As they project themselves onto this environment and observe the consequences, they learn about their identities in the world and the value of other entities in the world.

In other words, sensemaking is a feedback process in which individuals become aware of their identity due to the mutual influence of others. Participants use this process to extract cues for making decisions on what information is relevant and what explanations are acceptable (Brown et al. 2007). Extracted cues provide links to what may be occurring (Weick 1995). We should note that this process takes advantage of subjectivity, not just objective analysis or a clear understanding of the situation. Therefore, users of the sensemaking approach favor plausibility over accuracy in accounts of events and contexts. Ideally, the empathetic understanding of other participants is coupled with a high level of intelligence to understand the causality and scenarios of events in the past and in the future. We can think of sensemaking as a process that is available to people who have sufficiently developed their own modes of intelligence and emotion.

In information science, sensemaking is approached a little differently. (For clarity, here we unify Sense Making and sense-making into "sensemaking.") As in the Wikipedia's chapter above on Sensemaking, Dervin (Dervin 1983, 1992) has investigated sensemaking experienced by individuals when attempting to make sense of observed data. In systems engineering and the analysis and synthesis of human factors, the concepts extracted and the theories obtained should be both measurable and testable. For this sake sensemaking enables us to investigate and improve the interaction between humans and information technologies, where humans play a significant role in adapting and responding to unexpected or unknown situations as well as to recognized ones.

A noteworthy point we lean from these studies on sensemaking cited from Wikipedia is that it is a process that is initiated when an individual or organization recognizes the inadequacy of their current understanding of events (Klein et al., 2006). Sensemaking is a two-way process of collecting data in a temporary frame and then fitting the frame around available data. The formation of frames and the revision of the data and the frame are intrinsically connected: the data evoke frames and these frames are used when sensing the valuable parts of an environment and selecting/connecting data. As in organization studies, this description resembles the model of metacognitive processes that are used by both individuals and groups to build, verify, and modify scenarios with situational awareness and can be extended to account for an unrecognized situation which may appear in the future. We technically realized chance discovery as mentioned later that is conceptually quite close to sensemaking/Sensemaking as early as 2000, independently of studies introduced above (Ohsawa and Fukuda 2002; Ohsawa and McBurney 2003). However, we should say they still provide us with fundamental reasons why human- and process-centric approach works for chance discoveries as mentioned later, and why the approach can be realized by the Innovators Marketplace in this book.

2.3   Innovation as Interactive Value-Sensing with Insight

When we read about innovators in history, and when we meet people creating ideas in business, there are certain patterns that appear common to the moment of insight, i.e., finding latent values via breaking the *impasse*. We can define insight as the introduction of a novel variable that solves a posed problem satisfying a set of constraints by escaping from an impasse. By impasse here we mean being trapped in a local optima where some part of the problem is unsolved or some constraints are unsatisfied. For example, following the experiment by Terai and Miwa (Terai and Miwa 2003), let us try to solve the problem of finding a co-relation between the values of x, y, and z, where the sequence of (x, y, z) has been observed in the order of time as

$$(0, 1, 1), (1, 3, 4), (5, 2, 7), (0, 0, 0), (1, 1, 3), \ldots \qquad (2.1)$$

Here, we normally hypothesize the linear equation "$z = x + y$" based on the first four triples, and get confused with the fifth because 3 is not equal to $1 + 1$. We are trapped by the simple constraints, or the bias, due to our implicit belief that we should find the relationship between the given three variables and that the correlation should be simple-ideally, linear. What would happen if we abandoned this belief?

One thing to try would be introducing a new variable, u, which takes the value of 0 until the fourth triple and 1 after the fifth. This enables us to make the new hypothesis that z is the last digit of the sum of x, y, and u. Then, let us continue the following sequence that appears with the passing of time as

$$(3, 2, 6), (5, 3, 9), (1, 0, 2), (3, 3, 5), \ldots \qquad (2.2)$$

Here again, with the fourth (the ninth from the very first of the sequence), we find ourselves in error because 5 is not equal to $3 + 3 + 1$. At last, we find that we have been tricked by our own common sense into feeling that z should be a function of the variables including x and y. By excluding this constraint, we can introduce a new variable, t (time), which is not really new but of which we have been previously unaware. That is, z is just a linear function increasing by three every time z is equal to the third digit of $3t - 2$.

In this example, we created or became aware of an essential underlying variable to explain observed facts with/by excluding constraints. If the reader feels the above example is irrelevant to innovation, let us change from the triple of (x, y, z) to ("*x!: the daily number of people who eat at the sushi bar close to the station,*" "*y!: the daily number of people who drink at the pub close to the station,*" and "*z!: the daily number of passengers who disembark at the station*").

Suppose the values of these variables are collected every day by the station's data center. If x' plus y' looks close to z', it may look like people who disembark at the station are interested in drinking or eating. However, in a few days, we may find that z' is increasing while x' and y' are both decreasing. Thus, we should consider other variables that govern the behaviors of the passengers. After a couple of days, the increase in the number of passengers comes out to be radical, which makes us aware of a hidden factor like u, as we mentioned above. This is how we come to highlight an event that we had not noticed until then: the town had suddenly become famous for the discovery of a hot spring. In this scenario, we should find a way to link the station with the hot spring, such as by selling discount tickets for visitors to the spa or making a specially designed coach for elderly people who may become repeat customers of the spa. Such new designs result in an innovation, for not only this area but also for other areas with underlying hot springs.

2.4   Auxiliary Lines as Signs of Insight in Interpreting Images

In order to show the fundamental cognitive model of insight, here we show evidence of eye movements connecting important parts of a presented image. The movement of eyes has been shown to be a key factor in human decision making, for example, in consumers' brand choices (Pieters and Warlop 1999;Pieters et al. 2002;Pieters and Wedel 2004). When customers in a supermarket are looking at commodities on a shelf, their view may be focused on something they have been unconsciously looking for. Therefore, by investigating eye movement, we should be able to determine the unconscious interests of customers.

There have been significant advances in the study of eye movement in recent years. The basic models have been developed on the basis of the amount of time spent fixating on an object (Just and Carpenter 1980; Rayner 1995). Methods for automating the protocol for analyzing eyes have also been developed using the cognitive models of fixation and object tracking (Salvucci and Anderson 1998).

Cognitive scientists link eye movement to high-level (intelligent) information processing. Terai and Miwa discovered that the direction of eye movement changes discontinuously when insight occurs, i.e., when an individual overcomes an impasse. For example, Fig. 2.1 shows a table of various digits placed in the cells, forming lines that are scrolled up with time. This table was shown to participants wearing eye-tracking glasses who were instructed to look at the table and search for a pattern ruling the values in the three numbers in each line, e.g., "$x + y = z$." They were then asked to utter which number they were thinking about each time (Terai and Miwa 2003).

In this experiment, insight meant the release from the blocking hypothesis, i.e., from an impasse due to the artificial constraint "$x + y = z$," where participants first tried to interpret the rule underlying the first three lines. The results showed that an insight causes a discontinuous change in the movement of eyes. Eye movement was in the horizontal direction when a participant was saying "maybe $x + y = z$, but the fourth line violates this rule …." However, when the participant found the correct rule, i.e., "$z_r = $ (the last digit of)$z_r - 1 + 3$" for all r, the eyes discontinuously changed their movement to the vertical direction. From this example, we conclude that eye movement signals a measure of *insight*, which is an essential cognitive effect for understanding the structure of a target problem.

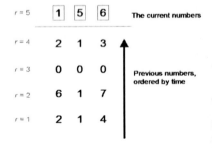

Fig. 2.1 Experiment to find the rule *underlying digits* (Terai and Miwa 2003). The digits are scrolling: the values of x, y, and z (the digits in the *left*, *central*, and *right* cells) in each line appear simultaneously, and new lines appear from the *bottom*

2.4.1 Vision, Attention, and Interpretation

To expand on these studies on eye movement, let us deal with the question of how a viewer interprets what is supposed to be an abstract image. For example, in his painting *Guernica*, it is thought that Picasso meant to convey that the air force attacked innocent people in the city, people and animals are dead on the road, and women are crying and hugging dead babies in their arms. Our point here is to investigate the human cognitive process when obtaining an interpretation, which is a hypothetical scenario, after an individual has viewed an image for a short time. That is, when individuals interpret an image, they create a hypothesis of an underlying scenario that may or may not correspond to the scenario imagined by the person who created the image. This can be regarded as an example of how an individual interprets an image that has been designed as the medium of a message.

Below, we discuss an experiment in which participants viewed images for a fixed length of time and we then investigated the fragments of messages they perceived. To quickly summarize the results in advance: A *slow saccade line* (SSL), a continuous line of eye movement that is as slow as the pursuit (a slow eye movement in pursuing a moving object, as stated later) but that occurs while gazing at a still image, partially corresponds with the viewer's interpretation of the image. That is, *auxiliary lines* emerge in eye movements when interpreting an image.

Auxiliary lines are strongly linked to *chance discovery* (discussed in more detail in the next subsection), which has been studied as a topic for the development of methods to discover a *chance*: an event that may be significant in human decision making. A chance might be rare, and its meaning can be too uncertain to interpret from the observable part of the real world, so pure computational analysis for understanding a chance is difficult. In this sense, the human cognitive process in interpreting and understanding the meaning of a chance is the core issue in chance discovery.

Researchers on chance discovery have studied the perception of decision makers by interpreting maps of the co-occurrence among events in various types of real environments, such as supermarkets, textile exhibitions, risk evaluation in banks, product design, etc. Such maps are obtained by visualizing the co-occurrence of items representing events in data collected from a business environment (e.g., Ohsawa and Usui 2005; Goda and Ohsawa 2007; Horie et al. 2007). In the process of chance discovery, users follow four steps (Fig. 2.2) when presented with a map:

(1) Users perceive the existence of patterns of event-occurrence that are easy to understand (there are no conflicts with intuition).
(2) Users explore new scenarios by trying to connect the episodes corresponding to the patterns perceived in step (1).
(3) Users then identify a bridge, i.e., an event that rarely occurs in the data but may be relevant to multiple episodes.
(4) Users have an "aha!" moment and perceive a meaningful combination of episodes via the bridge, creating a scenario they can then use as a guideline for

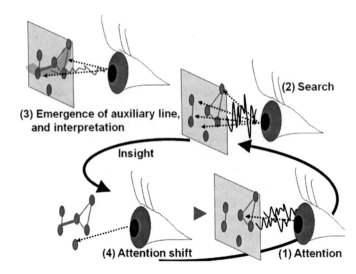

Fig. 2.2 Human cognitive process for interpreting an image by identifying auxiliary (bridging) lines

choosing actions in the future. In other words, they create a new plan of action by connecting episodes and bridges in the visualized map. After this plan is created, users shift their attention back to the map and return to step (1).

In step (1), users might be trapped in an impasse posed by cognitive constraints that could force them to consider only common-sense episodes corresponding to patterns. In steps (2)–(4), users are released from the constraint and create new scenarios. We expect this process model (in other words, the imagination of underlying scenarios) to also work for human interpretation of images such as artwork and commercial posters, not just puzzling event maps or scrolling tables. For steps (2) and (3), users should find auxiliary lines (Ohsawa and Maeda 2008, 2009) between basic patterns that equip them with effective clues for creating scenarios. In the experiment below, we instructed ten participants to look at images that were new to them: four abstract paintings by Pablo Picasso.

2.4.2 Experiment

We showed ten participants (two groups of five) abstract images with meanings that are said to be difficult to interpret but possible to understand once explained. The images were photographs of pictures by Pablo Picasso. One of them, shown in Fig. 2.3, is a photograph of the central part of the large picture *Guernica*, an artwork on warfare. The participants could not explain the artist's intended meaning ("*the scene of an air-force attack*") in preliminary interviews (we selected participants who were unfamiliar with this famous painting).

Fig. 2.3 The center-part of Pablo Picasso's *Guernica*

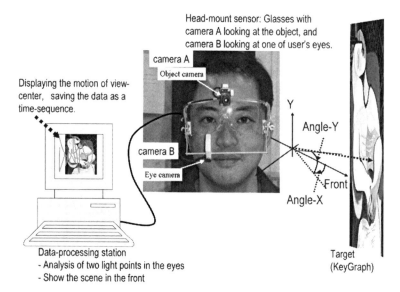

Fig. 2.4 The eye-movement sensing system (FreeView glasses)

The pictures were placed 1.5 m away from the participant. Each participant wore FreeView glasses (Fig. 2.4) produced by Takei Scientific Instruments Co. Ltd. These glasses are part of the most widely used eye-movement sensing system in Japan. In this system, eye-track data can be obtained as long as the view angle is within 20° from the center of the sight, with a sampling rate of once per 0.033 s. The movement of the eyes to the target was obtained and is indicated by the curves on the left-hand side of Fig. 2.4. We ensured that the target images, which were 0.5×0.5 mm in size, stayed in the 20° range by placing them 1.5 m in front of the participant's eyes.

2.4.3 Results

First, let us focus on one participant. The eye movements during the 3 min he was looking at *Guernica* are shown in Figs. 2.5, 2.6, and 2.7. The number above each picture means where the participant is in the steps after he started looking at the image, where 30 corresponds to 1 s. For example, "2,500–3,500" in Fig. 2.5 means that the dots in this figure represent eye movements from 1.5 to 2.0 min after the viewing started.

In the case of this participant, the eye movement started from two parts of *Guernica*: the face of the horse on the left and the people on the right. This attention lasted for about 2 min. Next, the eyes quickly traced a line connecting the horse face and the people, as shown in Fig. 2.6. This line was then revisited and reinforced, i.e., the eyes focused on the line connecting the right and left parts of the picture, as shown in Fig. 2.7.

We say that the line was "revisited and reinforced" because we found a dramatic change in the eye movement between Figs. 2.6 and 2.7. The velocity of the participants' eyes decreased, especially for the last 6.7 s, which was just before the participant's insightful comment, "This picture looks like a war, probably an air force attack." An interesting phenomenon was that the participant could not explain why he finally reached this interpretation. However, when we showed him

◆ 2500–3500

Fig. 2.5 Eye movement from 1.5 to 2.0 min after starting to look at Guernica

◆ 3500–4500

Fig. 2.6 Eye movement from 2.0 to 2.5 min after starting to look at Guernica

◆ 4500–5500
◇ 5300–5500

Fig. 2.7 Eye movement for the final 36.7 s (*white dots* show the final 6.7 s)

the eye-track (Fig. 2.7), he said "The object in the hand of the citizen is a lamp, and the one at the top of the picture may be a bomb ... killing the horse and soldiers! The two citizens on the right-hand side needed the light of the lamp, because after the bomb attack the city was dark."

Let us categorize different types of eye movement when fixated on a still object in the conventional manner, as follows:

- *A (slow) drift*: A low-velocity movement taking place invariantly, of about 5 min of view angle.
- *A tremor*: A high-frequency tremble of 1 min width, mostly co-occurring with drifts.
- *A micro-saccade, or flick*: A stepwise movement ranging up to 20 min.

When the target of attention moves, the eye movements are classified on the basis of the viewer's attention type. These types correspond to different velocities of eye movement:

- *Saccade* (50° or 60–600°/s): A large swing that occurs when the viewer shifts the target of attention. Intentional shifts of attention are reflected to saccade.
- *Pursuit* (5–30°/s): Middle-velocity movement that occurs when looking at a moving object.

Let us compare the phenomena in our experiment with these known patterns. The eyes, for the last 6.7 s just before insight (Fig. 2.7), after the earlier periods (Figs. 2.5 and 2.6) trying to interpret *Guernica*, moved at a velocity of 10–40°/s, which is slower than an ordinary saccade, but faster than the range of pursuit (5–30°/s). Note that all the images in the experiment were still. Although some quick movements, as fast as saccade, were observed, the participants' utterances about their impressions often occurred with slower velocity eye movement. A possible explanation of this exceptional velocity may be that the participant is searching for evidence to support the scenario that he/she has thought about for each local part of the picture. In other words, the movement in the last 6.7 s may have been a series of intentional saccades, the swift length (and accordingly the velocity also) of which has been reduced so that it can fit the restricted local area of attention focus.

We can infer that this participant found the lines (by which Picasso is said to have meant light rays) radiating from what he called the bomb and the lamp and connected them to the people on the right of the picture, thus forming a meaningful structure. Similar phenomena occurred in our experiments with other Picasso pictures. Let us call such a line, where the eyes move slowly to form a meaningful scenario by connecting parts on the way, a *slow saccade line* (SSL). We performed experiments to validate our hypothesis that SSL reflects the human process to reach the interpretation of a target image, the results of which have been published in a previous work (Ohawa and Maeda 2008).

Scan paths, which are lines that connect the major components of a picture, are said to play an essential role in the human cognition of artwork (Norton and Stark 1971). However, the results of the experiment described above imply that some small part of the scan can be regarded as an auxiliary line for combining components of the target image to achieve the externalization of a meaningful structure. We find SSL-like movements in the literature relevant to the shift of covert (implicit) attention, until acquiring overt (explicit) attention where sense organs are directed to a stimuli source (Hoffman and Subramaniam 1995; Peterson et al. 2004). The experimental results above may be regarded as an evidence of the process to reach an explicit attention to an image embracing a meaningful story, where eyes reveal the story before the mouth.

Let us summarize this section about eye movement. Sequential changes in eye movement can be interpreted as evidence of the participant's attention process. First participants pay attention to parts of an image that are easier to interpret, which in *Guernica* are the eyes of the horse and of the inhabitants of the city, and then they search for and find bridges to connect these basic parts. The emergent interpretation of the figure may further be reinforced by slow eye movement at a velocity and shape close to SSL that follows the bridge above, as in the 6.7 s just before the insight of the viewer of *Guernica*. Eyes can also move relatively slowly (less than 60°/s, which is incomparably slower than an ordinary saccade) along SSLs. Steps (1), (2), and (3) in the process model we presented in Fig. 2.2 are evident in such cases.

Furthermore, looking a one's own eye-track lines urges the mind to think of the reasons behind an interpretation, which can be regarded as an effect of metacognition.

2.5 Summary

Our findings show that individuals subjectively externalize the latent meaning underlying an image by relating parts that are easy to see and understand. In other words, we relate things that are familiar to us with or via things that may be unfamiliar. Regardless of our accuracy, i.e., whether the externalized meaning corresponds to facts or to what the artist intended, the finding instills in us a sense of new value. We can thus conclude that value sensing results from the human cognition of visualized information that includes both familiar and unfamiliar parts by making latent connections. The process of sensemaking as a methodology for elevating and using the sense of value provides hints for realizing the value-sensing lifestyle of people in communities. The methods and techniques of chance discovery we have been developing since 2000 can also be positioned as a way to develop and utilize data visualization tools that take advantage of the nature of human insight and apply them to business-oriented processes that can be explained by theories on sensemaking. Because the methods of chance discovery form the essential base for the Innovators' Marketplace, the core concept of this book, we will now present cases of chance discovery in actual business scenarios.

References

Brown AL (1987) Metacognition, executive control, self-regulation, and other more mysterious mechanisms. In: Weinert FE, Kluwe RH (eds) Metacognition, motivation, and understanding. Lawrence Erlbaum Associates, Hillsdale, pp 65–116

Brown AD, Stacey P, Nandhakumar J (2007) Making sense of sensemaking narratives. Hum Relat 61(8):1035–1062

Cohen, MS, Freeman JT, Wolf S (1996) Meta-recognition in time-stressed decision making: recognizing, critiquing, and correcting. J Hum Fact Ergon Soc 38(2):206–219

Dervin B (1983) An overview of sense-making research: concepts , methods and results. In: Proceedings of the annual meeting of the international communication association, Dallas, 1983

Dervin B (1992) From the mind's eye of the user: the sense-making qualitative-quantitative methodology. In: Glazier JD, Powell RR (eds) Qualitative research in information management. Libraries Unlimited, Englewood, pp 61–84

Donaldson M (1992) Human minds: an exploration, allen. The Penguin Press, Lane

Dunford R, Jones D (2000) Narrative in strategic change. Hum Relat 53:1207–1226

Flavell JH (1987) Speculations about the nature and development of metacognition. In: Weinert FE, Kluwe RH (eds) Metacognition, motivation and understanding. Lawrence Erlbaum Associates, Hillside, pp 21–29

Goda S, Ohsawa Y (2007) Estimation of chain reaction bankruptcy structure by chance discovery method with time order methods and directed KeyGraph. J Syst Sci Syst Eng 489–498

Hoffman J, Subramaniam B (1995) The role of visual attention in saccadic eye movements. Percept Psychophys 57:787–795

Horie K, Maeno Y, Ohsawa Y (2007) Data crystallization applied to desinging new products. J Syst Sci Syst Eng 16(1):34–49

Isabella LA (1990) Evolving interpretations as change unfolds: how managers construe key organizational events. Acad Manage J 33(1):7–41

Just MA, Carpenter PA (1980) A theory of reading: from eye fixations to comprehension. Psychol Rev 87:329–335

Klein G, Moon B, Hoffman RF (2006) Making sense of sensemaking II: a macrocognitive model. IEEE Intell Syst. 21(5):88–92

Norton D, Stark L (1971) Eye movements and visual perception. Sci Am 224:34–43

Ohsawa Y, Fukuda H (2002) Chance discovery by stimulated group of people – An application to understanding rare consumption of food. J Conting Crisis Manag 10(3):129–138

Ohsawa Y, Maeda Y (2008) Slow saccade lines in eye-track as units of semantic cognition, poster abstract. In: The 30th annual meeting of the cognitive science society (CogSci08), Washington, 2008

Ohsawa Y, Maeda Y (2009) Eyes draw auxiliary lines in interpreting images. J Comput. 4(10):1012–1021

Ohsawa Y, McBurney P (eds) (2003) Chance discovery. Springer, New York

Ohsawa Y, Usui M (2005) Creative marketing as application of chance discovery. In: Ohsawa Y, Tsumoto S (eds) Chance discoveries in real world decision making. Springer, New York, pp 253–272

Peterson MS, Kramer AF, Irwin DE (2004) Covert shifts of attention precede involuntary eye movements. Percept Psychophys 66:398–405

Pieters R, Warlop L (1999) Visual attention during brand choice: the impact of time pressure and task motivation. Int J Res Mark 16(1):1–16

Pieters R, Warlop L, Wedel M (2002) Breaking through the clutter: benefits of advertisement originality and familiarity for brand attention and memory. Manage Sci 48(6):765–781

Pieters R, Wedel M (2004) Attention capture and transfer in advertising: brand, pictorial, and text-size effects. J Mark 68(2):36–50

Rayner K (1995) Eye movements and cognitive processes in reading, visual search, and scene perception. In: Findlay JM, Walker R, Kentridge RW (eds) Eye movement research: mechanisms, processes, and applications. Elsevier Science, New York

Salvucci DD, Anderson JR (1998) Tracing eye movement protocols with cognitive process models. In: Proceedings of the twentieth annual conference of the cognitive science society, Hillsdale, 1998, pp 923–928

Suwa M (2008) A cognitive model of acquiring embodied expertise through meta-cognitive verbalization. Inform Media Technol 3(2):399–408

Terai H, Miwa K (2003) Insight problem solving from the viewpoint of constraint relaxation using eye movement analysis. In: Proceedings of the 4th international conference of cognitive science, Tehran, 2003, pp 671–676

Thompson E (2001) Empathy and consciousness. J Conscious Stud 8(5–7):1–32

Weick K (1979) The social psychology of organizing. McGraw-Hill, New York

Weick K (1995) Sensemaking in organisations. Sage, London

Weick K, Sutcliffe KM, Obstfeld D (2005) Organizing and the process of sensemaking. Organ Sci 16(4):409–421

Watson TJ (1995) Rhetoric, discourse and argument in organizational sensemaking: a reflexive tale. Organ Stud 16(5):805–821

Watson TJ (1998) Managerial sensemaking and occupational identities in Britain and Italy: the role of management magazines in the process of discursive construction. J Manag Stud 35(3):285–301

Chapter 3
Using Maps for Scenario Externalization

3.1 Chance Discovery and Innovation

Successful companies understand and respond to the latent demands of customers. "Chance discovery" means, as stated previously, the discovery of events essential for making decisions (Ohsawa and McBurney 2003). In this chapter, we describe a method of chance discovery in which visual/touchable tools for data-based decision making are positioned in the spiral of human–machine collaboration in a business environment. We present a case of an actual business using this method to choose the most promising textile products for production and sale in the real market. The results are evaluated on the basis of the subjective criteria of business people rather than the objective criteria of a computer, and the evaluation is then passed on to the next cycle in the process of chance discovery, thereby improving the business performance.

In the various projects we facilitated with companies, teams working on marketing, product design, services, etc. acquired a new awareness of the important parts of their market that they had not previously taken into account. We used the KeyGraph®[1] algorithm to create a diagram of correlations between products and customer behaviors, which we then presented to business people as a map of the market. This map featured (1) clusters of items frequently preferred by the same user, and (2) items that bridged the clusters, indicating that they may correspond to a latent market demand coming up in the near future. In this chapter, we show a couple of examples of the diagrams obtained by KeyGraph being used to assist with chance discovery in actual business situations.

---

[1] KeyGraph® is registered trademark of Yukio Ohsawa of the University of Tokyo, Japan.

Y. Ohsawa and Y. Nishihara, *Innovators' Marketplace*, Understanding Innovation,
DOI 10.1007/978-3-642-25480-2_3, © Springer-Verlag Berlin Heidelberg 2012

3.2 Using Chance Discovery in Business Planning

A primary cause of failure in business is business planners' inability to keep up with the changing demands of customers (Fine 1998). The traditional make-up of some companies can prevent planners from making the creative decisions required to survive in a dynamic market. In this sense, there is a clear need for *chance discovery* techniques (Ohsawa and McBurney 2003; Ohsawa and Fukuda 2002) – methods of determining which events are significant for a given decision and of managing these events to enable creative decisions and actions to take place. In this section, we show a case in which users executed a method of chance discovery and management in a company that produces and sells textiles. The method was comprised of the three factors below. Factors (2) and (3) are a part of factor (1).

(1) The process of chance discovery using the *double helix* (Ohsawa 2003a) model, where a group of collaborating workers progressively become more deeply interested in detecting new chances.
(2) A visual map of the market (obtained by KeyGraph (Ohsawa 2003b)) applied to the market data with real pieces of textile on corresponding nodes.
(3) A marketing meeting to create marketing scenarios corresponding to paths on the visual map, where candidates of chances are detected at the crosspoints of scenarios and discussed.

A computer objectively visualized commercial items and then participants, motivated by subjective interest in the items, would discuss them, reflect, and finally propose scenarios. As a result, the company was able to externalize the potential value of new items and ultimately to successfully sell them. In terms of marketing, we aimed to achieve at least the following two goals.

(1) To strengthen the sensitivity of marketers to unusual events, e.g., the purchase of a new item by a customer, that may have a big impact on the market so long as marketers do not overlook the value of the event. A computer is not very good at evaluating the significance of new or unusual events because the causes and effects of such events tend to be unknown and because there are almost no examples of unknown causes in recorded data.

There is a possibility that, in the past, hidden causal events have appeared to marketers because they continuously keep in touch with the market. However, it might not be possible to express some types of tacit memory in speech or in a written document. In such cases, it is necessary to externalize the marketer's tacit feeling of value. However, if a marketer relies only on his/her own experiences, there is a risk of overlooking essential customer behaviors because one's recollection of past experiences is restricted to a specified part of the market. Therefore, we require an abstract map of the market that visualizes the positions of various products and customer behaviors in order to externalize the experiences of experts (marketers here) without a strong bias due to personal frame of recollection. Here, a graph including *islands* (products of established popularity) and *bridges* (weak correlations between islands) in the market, visualized by KeyGraph, is shown as the map of the market. In order to stimulate the recollection of marketers, we further reinforced KeyGraph into a new device called a *touchable KeyGraph* on which real pieces of textile items are put so that users can physically feel the sensation of the textile.

(2) To keep individuals motivated to discover and manage chances in their organization. Generally speaking, persuasion, i.e., getting the members of a company to agree to a proposal, is difficult if the proposal hinges on taking advantage of a rare or unusual event. This is because the future of a rare event is uncertain, and if individuals do not know much about an event they tend to consider it untrustworthy. One way to motivate these suspicious individuals is to have them share their interests, choose and propose alternative scenarios, and work on their own decisions. In our work, we used group meetings, starting from interest-sharing and scenario-exchanging using the KeyGraph, to address continuous concerns.

3.3   The Double Helix Process of Chance Discovery for Innovative Decisions

In the double helix (DH) process of chance discovery, a computer helps deepen an individual's interest in a chance by continuously visualizing the interaction between individual and environment and between individual and individual (Ohsawa 2003a). Individuals and automated data mining tool(s) collaborate, each progressing in a spiral toward the creation of future events and actions, as in Fig. 3.1.

The DH model has two helical (spiral) sub-processes. One is of an individual's progression to deeper interest in chances. The other is of a computer's receiving, mining, and visualizing of the data (data mining: DM). In Fig. 3.1, the wide road depicts the process of individuals(s) and the dotted curve of the computer. Between these two helixes, interactions occur following the thin arrows in Fig. 3.1.

First, the object data (the data from the user's environment) are collected reflecting the user's interest in the target domain and put in the computer. The result of mining the object data (DM-b) is then applied to the user's understanding of scenarios, i.e., possible stories formed with events including potential chances. The subject data (the text record of the user's thoughts and communications about scenarios forthcoming in the future) is then put into the computer. The result of mining the subject data (DM-a) is shown to the user(s) to enable him, her, or them to mentally clarify the future scenario. This is essential because users tend to overlook their own ideas if their thoughts are not recorded. Even raw subject data, presented without being processed by data/text mining or visualization, often works for this purpose. The term *double helix* means the parallel and collaborative running of a pair of helixes (spiral processes) due to monitoring both the object data and subject data.

Our first step in the execution of DH was to have the marketing staff become interested in discovering chances. If we take Louis Pasteur's belief that "chance favors the prepared mind" and apply it to the collective mind of a group of

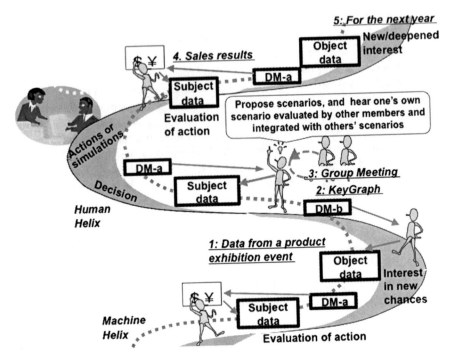

Fig. 3.1 The double helix (DH) model of chance discovery process

individuals in a team, we can say that "chance favors a group with a shared interest about chances." In order to ensure a properly prepared mind, we first educated the textiles marketing staff by explaining the potential value of rare events (in general terms rather than related to specific products or events) in a dynamic market. Then, to make sure they maintained their interest, we initiated a scenario communication activity in which the marketing staff were encouraged to talk about business scenarios that may have been executed previously or might be executed in the future. The members then proposed scenarios that dealt with both frequent and rare customer behaviors, eventually coming up with a scenario designed to lead the company to success. If any proposal carried the risk of failure, it could be rejected because. After all, the proposed scenarios came to be reflected to the product development and selling actions of the company. To summarize, the members' concerns were shared, combined, and solidified until they achieved a hit in the market.

3.4   Preliminary Comparison of Tools for Visual Data Mining

After the participants acquired interest during the DH process, object data related to the creation of new products to meet the demands of customers were visualized with data mining/visualizing tools. We had three members of the marketing staff evaluate

Fig. 3.2 Item-set data in the
order card of one customer

<Customer P's choice>
Item X: cotton,4way,...(features of item X)
Item Y: cotton,1way,...(features of item Y)
Item Z: rayon,4way,...(features of item Z)

three different tools for the same data of customers' orders in a product exhibition. It is true that three is quite a small number, but this was a preliminary step in an actual business project, and as such costs had to be kept as low as possible.

The object data were collected in the manner shown in Fig. 3.2, recording the textile selections all customers from 400 sample items (products including those not yet sold in the market) on display at a textile exhibition. Note that these data were chosen from among other kinds of data (such as sales figures) so that the company could deal with the potential of products that were not yet on the market.

To externalize the tacit dimension of the marketers' experience, the marketing staff (and the first author Ohsawa) had a discussion to reach a consensus about which tool would be best to visualize the following parts of the market.

(1) Islands, each of which correspond to a set of items that satisfy a certain existing desire of customers. These islands show popular (i.e., well-known to both staff and customers) components of the market.
(2) Bridges between the islands, which aid users' interpretation of customers' dynamic behaviors, such as shifts to/from islands. In contrast to existing marketing methods that assume each customer stays on one island, we seek triggers that prompt customers to seek new islands.

Clustering methods such as bottom-up (Han and Kamber 2001; Roussopoulos et al. 1995), hierarchical (Lance and Williams 1967), and strategies to cut bridges (Matsuo and Ohsawa 2002) do not work with our approach because they hide bridges. In the textile company, the marketing staff compared three tools: decision tree learning (Quinlan 1993), correspondence analysis (Greenacre 1993), and KeyGraph (Ohsawa 2003b) because these were regarded as satisfying (1) and (2) above. As we showed in Chap. 2, visual information satisfying these conditions is expected to be perceived by a human's vision and to enable the recognition of latent scenarios.

We created a decision tree in which a group of items with similar features was depicted as one node and the hierarchical relations between nodes were shown as a tree (a part is shown in Fig. 3.3). This structure was obtained by using the C4.5 algorithm on the features of items in the order-card data (Fig. 3.2). The marketers decided that a node in a higher level could be regarded as a bridge. However, when we did this, all the tendencies that emerged were already known to them, and no new findings were obtained even though we varied the parameters to include rare patterns. This is because IF-THEN rules such as "the product is ordered IF the price was more than 760 yen and the particularity was HMS" is stereotyped in the textile marketing field and therefore not meaningful in terms of providing new knowledge for creating new products (even though, as the marketing experts mentioned, they may be useful for educating new marketers).

price > 760
| particularity = HMS: ordered more than twice
| particularity = MMO
| | construction = DOUBLECLOTH: ordered more than twice
| particularity = standard
| | width(cm) > 113
| | | width(cm) <= 115
| | | | construction = SATTEN: ordered more than twice

Fig. 3.3 A decision tree, having learned the class of frequently bought items by C4.5

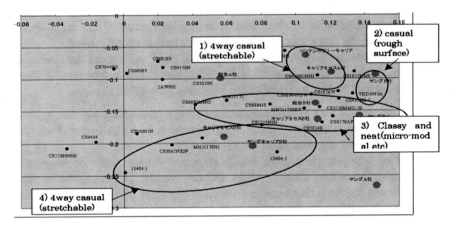

Fig. 3.4 A result of the correspondence analysis. The interpretations in the ellipses and labels *1)–4)* were made by the marketers

In the correspondence analysis, items and companies appearing in the same order-cards (as in Fig. 3.2) were located close to each other in the 2D visualization (as in Fig. 3.4). For example, CS3060HJ and CS4100NHJ in the circle of "1) 4-way casual" in Fig. 3.4 often appeared in the same order-card, meaning that many customers ordered these two items at the same time. The marketers said they recognized a group of neighboring items as an island and the nodes located between islands as a bridge. However, they felt it was difficult to interpret the bridge nodes, even though the clusters corresponded to typical loyal customers (discussed in more detail later).

In contrast, the KeyGraph map showed frequent items as black nodes (as in Fig. 3.5) and connected a pair of black nodes with solid black lines if they corresponded to a pair of items appearing frequently in the same order card. Islands in this map were shown as connected graphs of solid lines. Red (gray in this book) nodes denote rare items appearing in the same order cards as items in multiple islands. The dotted lines between red nodes and the islands are bridges. The final KeyGraph graph was considered as the map of the market.

In order to choose one (or more) tool from among the three, three executive members who worked in marketing strategy looked at the results and evaluated

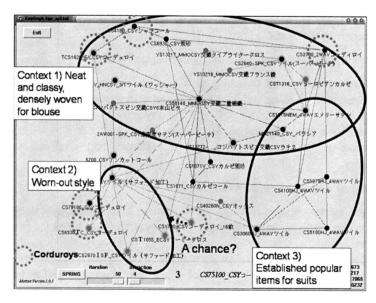

Fig. 3.5 KeyGraph result for the textile exhibition. Two islands formed, one including contexts *1*) and *3*) and the other corresponding to context *2*). The marketers paid attention to the bridge nodes in the *dotted circles*, but the "chance" was not discovered before the communication phase

the performance of each tool by writing scenarios about customer behaviors as interpreted from the graphs. These marketers satisfied the condition that the viewer have a rich enough knowledge of the market to understand all the items in the graph. Here, note that the performance of chance discovery depends on whether or not beneficial decisions can be obtained in the group discussions that come after this preliminary step, i.e., during communication about scenario proposals in the DH process. In the case of big organizations such as this one, an evaluation of the process of chance discovery must include how successfully the proposals can elicit a consensus about future actions among the leaders of the company, rather than how precisely the output corresponds to the past. This point is similar to the vision of sensemaking we introduced in Chap. 2. These particular marketers were selected because they had the most expertise and leadership ability.

Let us show a few scenarios interpreted by using each tool. The customers we mention are from companies that produce clothing from the materials sold by this textile company.

(Summary of scenarios based on decision trees)

- Most customers preferred to buy expensive textiles rather than low-cost ones because they like to produce stylish clothing to attract new consumers.
- Many customers preferred to mix double-woven and satin materials. This was in line with our understanding.

- Customers tended to buy denim textiles. This trend seems to have remained constant over the years.

(Summary of scenarios based on correspondence analysis)

- Most customers tended to belong to one of two major islands of preference: producing neat clothing styles and producing worn-out-looking casual clothing styles.
- Customer A preferred materials for classy clothes.
- Customer B preferred four-way woven materials and produced women's clothing.

(Summary of scenarios based on KeyGraph)

- Many customers bought items on one of the two islands (neat style or worn-out style). The marketers interpreted the three contexts in Fig. 3.5 as the essence of the two islands.
- The nodes on bridges are rare items and tended to be higher-cost versions of items on the islands. It might be a good idea to sell a regular textile and its high-cost equivalent in one set.

The output of KeyGraph was the closest to our aim of showing bridges in the market externalizing latent scenarios that correspond to connections via bridges. The other two methods worked only to confirm knowledge that had already been established.

3.4.1 Quantitative Comparison of Tool Performance

The evaluation criteria here are the ability of the tools to aid user creativity when developing scenarios. In Table 3.1, criterion (1) is the number of items in the output that the marketers regarded as items belonging to islands (i.e., items that were already popular) divided by the number of all items appearing in the output. These items were annotated by the marketers (e.g., the circular frames in Figs. 3.4 and 3.5). Criterion (2) is the number of items in the output that matched the

Table 3.1 Comparison of the three tools

Criterion	Correspondence analysis	Decision trees	KeyGraph
(1) Rate of items with explicit known demands	56%	60%	58%
(2) Rate of items relevant to latent demands	1%	3.3%	7.5%
(3) Number of feasible new scenarios	0	1	4
(4) Number of feasible scenarios via bridges	0	0	3
(5) Number of scenarios to beneficially change business strategies	0	1	3

customers' demands (but were not noticed before looking at the map) divided by the number of all items in the output. Criterion (3) is the number of proposed scenarios that are feasible in an actual business situation but that have not been proposed before. Criterion (4) is the number of scenarios, including the items of (2), amongst the scenarios in (3). Finally, criterion (5) is the number of scenarios that can be expected to create an innovation within the company. The marketers looked at these results and concluded that KeyGraph is the most suitable for creative business. All three tools could identify the established demands: the company could then satisfy customers with a stable supply of items that had proven popular by using tools with high values of criteria (1). The correspondence analysis was helpful in terms of satisfying individual customers using one-to-one marketing based on the preferences of each customer. However, KeyGraph enabled the marketers to identify customer demands that they had never noticed before, which in turn led them to think of new customer scenarios – the first step in creating an innovation.

3.5 Scenario Communication with Touchable KeyGraph

As Table 3.1 shows, KeyGraph was evaluated as the most useful for creative proposals fitting the market demand and for product development and promotion strategies. However, the connections among nodes via links in the graph tended to be too dense to interpret, especially when dealing with the large number of items the marketers wanted to see. This made it difficult to interpret the islands and bridges at a glance. The marketers overcame this problem by adding actual textile samples to the printed KeyGraph output (Fig. 3.6), thereby appealing to both the sense of touch and of sight. They used this touchable KeyGraph to recollect established fashions corresponding to the islands and to create new consumer scenarios by moving to and from the islands via bridges.

In the DH process (Fig. 3.1), the discussions that occur in group meetings are expected to trigger chance discovery for two reasons. First, if an individual has somebody to talk to, the proposed scenarios will be fed back to him or her after filtering out the meaningless parts, elaborating the meaningful parts, and correcting the misguided parts. In other words, the discussion results in a scenario being returned to the individual who originally proposed it with improvements brought about by objective evaluations and criticism. You can think of this as a supply and demand system, where subjects and data flow to and from each member of the group. Second, human communications may create stronger scenarios by combining proposed scenarios. For example, one of the marketers who was accustomed to dealing with customers in the contexts 1) and 3) (Fig. 3.5), i.e., business people, envisioned the following scenario:

Scenario 1: Business people wear smart suits made of densely woven fabric, but seek more casual clothes in order to feel relaxed.

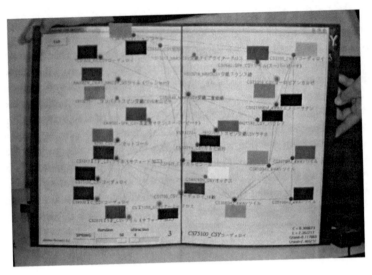

Fig. 3.6 The touchable KeyGraph with attached textile pieces

Another marketer who was more accustomed to context 2) (Fig. 3.5) proposed a slightly different scenario:

Scenario 2: Young people wear casual clothes, but sometimes seek neater ones.

After a 1-h discussion, another member, who had experience with the marketing of various kinds of textiles, proposed that business people wear neat suits but want to feel relaxed like young people on evenings and weekends. However, it is bothersome to change from a suit to casual clothes from top to bottom. Therefore, making a semi-casual, semi-business jacket, like the one in the center of Fig. 3.7, from the "chance" textile in Fig. 3.5, might be appealing to business people because all they have to do is to change the top to go out in the evening after work. Communication in a group of people with knowledge of different environmental contexts can thus lead to a consensus on a new scenario giving new meaning to an item that previously had been less popular than frequently ordered products.

3.5.1   Business Returns from the Chance Candidate

As mentioned above, the chance node between the "neat and classy" and "worn-out" clusters contributed to the creation of a business scenario that turned out to be extremely successful. In an autumn textile exhibition, the company exhibited textile samples to be used the following winter, including the items in Fig. 3.7. In terms of the number of orders, the chance node was ranked 52nd out of the 400 items exhibited. The textiles on the two islands and the chance node were sold as one set, and the customers (all of whom were in the business of producing and selling suits) were told that business people desire clothes to wear in their non-working hours.

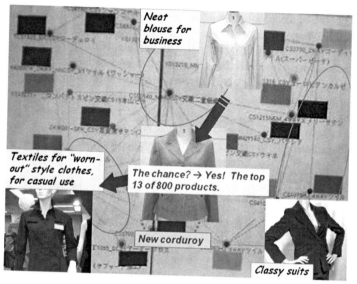

Fig. 3.7 Giving value to a "chance" candidate (see Fig. 3.5)

Table 3.2 Commercialized products and their sales ranking

Product	Rank in exhibition	Rank in sales
CS6930TC	52nd/400 items	13th/800 items
2AW001SPK	30th/400 items	28th/800 items
CS40260N	65th/400 items	24th/800 items
CS6930TC	52nd/400 items	33rd/800 items

The result was that the Corduroy (the chance node) was ranked 13th in a run-down of actual sales figures that winter among the 800 items sold by this company. It is so rare for a new product to rank higher than 30th that no such past record was found in their sales data. The rise from 52nd/400 in the exhibition to 13th/800 in the sales figures means that presenting a new scenario of consumer behavior stimulated a latent desire in consumers to introduce such a scenario to their lifestyles.

Let us now look at whether an awareness of novel consumer behavior scenarios, aided by chance discovery, can be generalized for other products. We looked at the sales figures of this textile company for five seasons: 2002 spring-to-summer (SS), 2002 autumn-to-winter (AW), 2003SS, 2003AW, and 2004SS. In each season, a map obtained by using KeyGraph was presented on which 30–50 nodes on islands and 5–10 nodes on bridges were shown. In total, they contained 240 nodes on islands and 32 on bridges.

To use the textiles in Table 3.2 as an example, the sales volume rank of new products corresponding to the chance-candidate (bridge) nodes chosen after group discussions was higher than that of their order frequency at the time of the exhibitions. These products were also shown to be superior to others: the sales rank of new products, i.e., products exhibited in the latest exhibition, ranged between

100th and 200th of the 800 items sold. In contrast, all the items that had been on the bridges and had been commercialized (promoted and sold after the exhibition) after using the chance discovery process ranked higher than 50th.

Conventional wisdom holds that set-sales, where items that often co-occur in the sales data are sold as one set with a reduced price, tend to increase the number of sales of each item in the set. However, the increased popularity of items on the bridges cannot be explained as the result of mere set-sales because other items were also sold in sets with closely positioned products in the correspondence analysis and the KeyGraph map. We conclude that the popularity spike was a direct result of using the process of chance discovery to come up with scenarios that were appealing to customers.

3.6   Summary of the Textile Company Case

Three phases – (1) getting users to focus on chances by educating them about chance discovery, (2) selecting object data and data mining tools, and (3) discussing scenarios as a group while looking at a market map-resulted in successful chance discovery.

The marketers adapted our KeyGraph to make it touchable and used it as a tool for visualizing the market map. The sales performance stemming from chances discovered using the proposed method was evaluated in terms of actual business gain. The cognitive tendency of humans to ignore events they know little about, which has been theoretically proposed in studies on causality (Evans 1987), came to life here in a case involving an actual business. The fact that data visualization enhances the creativity of a group is already well-known (Sumi and Mase 2003; Soukup 2002), but it is noteworthy here that, mid-process, the textile marketers extended the frame of visualization to include a touchable interface. This phenomenon shows that the process itself causes its own evolution. The case in the next section also demonstrates this self-evolutionary aspect in the sense that a new method for data visualization was suggested by users midway through the process. The new method that resulted from this suggestion forms the basis of the Innovators' Marketplace in the following chapters.

3.7   Data Crystallization for Scenarios Without Existing Events

3.7.1   The Challenge: Detecting Key Events that Have Zero Frequency in the Data

We first came up with our chance discovery method with the aim of detecting significant events for decision making via an understanding of the meanings of events, including rare ones, rather than identifying frequent patterns or patterns/rules for predicting rare events, as done in conventional data mining studies (Weiss and Hirsh 1998; Joshi 2002). However, the complexity of the real world is such that sometimes understanding it is beyond even the reach of chance discovery. For example, an innovative architect, who has never contacted a textile manufacturer directly (and so never appeared in the data of loyal customers), may come up with an idea of using textiles as material for the wall of a meeting room so that participants' voices sound soft. He orders some of the exhibited textiles to check their suitability for his purpose. Although no textile is perfect, the architect finally finds a good combination of textiles after dozens of experiments. In this case, the final product is a combination created by someone who is not even included in the loyal-customers list, and which never appears in the sales data. As in (von Hippel 2006), such innovation by lead users should not be ignored if the textile company is serious about creating innovation. This raises an important question: "How can we determine consumers' real and latent wants and requirements when we cannot find any data on them?" Individuals who use chance discovery and have gone through the spiral cycles usually acquire an awareness of invisible chances and therefore have to deal with this problem. This is where data crystallization comes into play: finding relevant ideas, events, and people when there is zero available data.

3.7.2 Naive KeyGraph Versus Data Crystallization

Let us explore the example of the architect from a market analysis point of view. The problem here is that there are missing links among products. The architect, who as you recall is unknown to the company, might make several different purchases of products in the clusters of textiles for jeans and for blouses. These submarkets may look superficially irrelevant when considering the demands of a customer who is an architect, but the elasticity of the jeans and the quick-dry nature of the blouses turns out to be perfect for the meeting room wall the architect wants to make. This makes the value of the missing link between the jeans and the blouse quite meaningful.

For the data in the target domain here, KeyGraph may show the relation of products on their co-occurrent frequencies. For example, in Eq. (3.1), let data D1 express a set of products, where each line represents one purchase by one customer. Here, product1 can be regarded as an event: one purchase. Regarding each item in the data as an event is meaningful when interpreting KeyGraph as a scenario map because a sequence of events on a path in the graph may be regarded as a reflection of some dynamic in the market.

$$D1 = product1, product2, product3$$
$$product1, product2, product3$$
$$product2, product1, product3, product6, product4$$
$$product5, product3$$
$$product6, product5$$

$$product5, product7, product8$$

$$product5, product6$$

$$product5, product7, product8$$

$$product7, product8, product6$$

$$product10, product9, product1, product8$$

$$product9, product10$$

$$product9, product10 \tag{3.1}$$

KeyGraph is then applied to D1. The results for two different parameter settings (the number of nodes and links) are shown in Fig. 3.8. Here, the appearance of a bridging product can become a central topic to the analysts. Three islands are obtained (including respective sets of product1, product2, product3, product5, product6, product7, product8, and product9, product10 for each of the two settings). The nodes and links on the islands show frequent purchases of product sets by the same customers, whereas the other lines (the lines linked to product4 in the left figure, and the larger number of lines in the right) show bridges. As you can see by comparing the right and left sides of the figure, a small change in the parameters results in a dramatic change to the structure of the graph. However, whichever setting the user may choose, the latent dynamics ruling the bridges among the islands cannot be clearly interpreted in either. For example, market analysts can use the graph on the left to make a customer behavior scenario, like "product1, product2, and product3 are bought by companies selling jeans, and product5, product6, product7, and product8 are bought by business apparel companies selling classy suits and blouses. For some reason, someone is buying both types of products, as shown by the dotted links coming from product4. Hmmm … What is the reason?" Further discussion of this graph might help to solve the mystery - for example, perhaps someone bought from both groups just by chance, or maybe it was done on purpose to achieve a specific goal, such as in the imaginary case of the architect who invented the new wall.

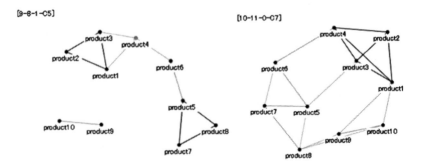

Fig. 3.8 KeyGraph output graphs for D1 using different parameter settings

We do not find any bridge between the islands of (product1, product2, product3) and (product9, product10). If we increase the number of linked nodes on each island, as on the right, the connections will be too complex to interpret.

We developed the data crystallization method in 2005, 7 years after KeyGraph, in response to KeyGraph users who wanted to identify chances that were not included in the data. Even though 7 years had passed, the only addition needed was a small step: visualizing the data by inserting artificial dummy items. These dummy items are unobservable events of an unknown entity and are not included in the given data. By using data crystallization, we can see an overview of the real world, complete with the potential existence of significant but hidden (unobservable/unknown) events. The mechanism behind this is similar to the crystallization of snow: a dummy item is a particle of dust connecting molecules of water in the air. The dust creates a bridge between the water molecules to form snow crystal, just as the structure of events in the data is formed by inviting a dummy node from another territory to act as a bridge for the substructures.

As a simple example, let us add dummy items to Eq. (3.1), which now becomes Eq. (3.2). A dummy item gets inserted into each line of D2 sufficed with the corresponding line number. KeyGraph is then applied to the data-set. Dummy items that appear on the bridges of the graph are highlighted (shown in red (gray in this book)) as in Fig. 3.9.

$$
\begin{aligned}
D2 = {} & product1, product2, product3, & & dummy1 \\
& product1, product2, product3, & & dummy2 \\
& product2, product1, product3, product6, product4, & & dummy3 \\
& product5, product3, & & dummy4 \\
& product6, product5, & & dummy5 \\
& product5, product7, product8, & & dummy6 \\
& product5, product6, & & dummy7 \\
& product5, product7, product8, & & dummy8 \\
& product7, product8, product6, & & dummy9 \\
& product10, product9, product1, product8, & & dummy10 \\
& product9, product10, & & dummy11 \\
& product9, product10, & & dummy12
\end{aligned}
$$

$$(3.2)$$

Some dummy nodes appear in the graph (Fig. 3.9), forming bridges between islands. Compared with the dotted lines in the left figure of Fig. 3.8, which just imply the existence of a hidden bridge between two clusters, Fig. 3.9 shows that an invisible bridge has been activated in several lines, including the tenth (the one

[9-8-5-C5]

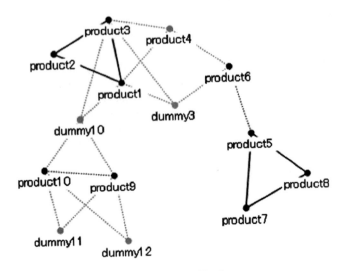

Fig. 3.9 Result of KeyGraph for D2: Output of data crystallization

corresponding to dummy10), and also that the latent demand connected products on the island of (product1, product2, product3) and of (product9, product10).

Although product8 is included in the tenth line along with product1, we can tell by looking at this data that product1 is so essential that it is connected to other products, such as product6, which is relevant to product8. Product8, meanwhile, belongs to the same group as product6 and product7. If product1 is the most elastic textile for jeans and the common feature of product9 and product10 is a quick drying time, the market analyst may notice that someone is interested in mixing the two features for some purpose. In order to solve this mystery (i.e., to notice the architect's demand), a discussion for scenario externalization is required.

3.8 Application of Data Crystallization to Innovations from Patent Documents

Here, let us present a case in which data crystallization was applied to the invention of new functions for a surface inspection system (SIS), a machine for detecting defects on couple charged devices (CCDs). As shown in Fig. 3.10, an SIS transports a CCD film on its conveyor belt and lights are shone from over and under the film. Cameras then take pictures of the reflected and penetrated lights and send the images to the computer. The computer runs image analysis software to detect and classify the defects (scratches, spots, etc.) into classes in order to understand what caused them.

Fig. 3.10 A surface inspection system (SIS) for a couple charged device (CCD)

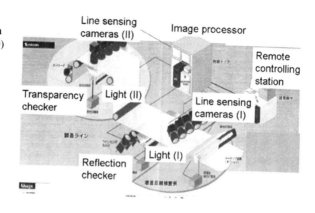

One problem in developing and improving this system was that the people on the development team come from different backgrounds and areas of expertise, including experts on cameras, lights, computer programming, and the conveyer belt system. This made it difficult for them to communicate with each other about the various technologies involved, and as a result they tended to confine themselves to their own thoughts. The problem, of course, was that they could not create or improve the SIS functions without a novel combination of their cumulative expertise.

As previously reported (Horie and Ohsawa 2006), the original DH-process method of chance discovery has been applied using KeyGraph to show the structure of words in the combined texts of business reports showing customer claims. In such a case, the text has to be dealt with as data in the same form as Eq. (3.1) by regarding each word as a product and each sentence as a basket (i.e., corresponding to a line in Eq. (3.1). As each staff member reported on the restricted focus of his/her domain, the islands in the obtained KeyGraph (as in Fig. 3.11) corresponded to established knowledge specific to those domains, and nodes showing rare words revealed a few bridges between these domains. The nodes at these bridges were words relating to some noteworthy aspect of the defects on the CCD film. The team members ultimately came to understand that combinations of technologies are required for the detection of fatal defects: for example, a defect called "spottiness" could be detected by combining the technologies of light and image analysis software. In the end, the company registered five new patents and developed a machine that became the highest-ranked SIS, simply by combining different spheres of knowledge.

However, they did not feel that this success was an innovation, because it was nothing more than making use of existing technologies to achieve the same purpose they always had. They therefore acquired a new goal, which was to attain sustainable leadership in the SIS market – not only by responding to the known claims of known customers but also by externalizing future demands and satisfying them by more creative combinations of technologies.

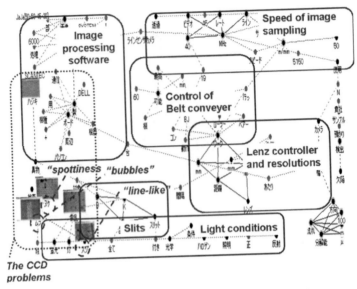

Fig. 3.11 The simple KeyGraph applied to designing a CCD scratch inspection system

To accomplish this goal, they now focused their attention on the rich public data on patents in technical domains relevant to SIS. This new dataset, however, was not easy to deal with by KeyGraph because, unlike business reports, each patent is described in words that are narrowly restricted to specific technical terms. The collection of patent documents seldom included bridging words such as "spottiness." Thus, in this case we applied data crystallization to discover hidden ideas underlying the dummy nodes that implied the latent existence of concepts bridging the islands.

We performed a preliminary test based on text created by combining documents related to six Japanese patents of marking systems for defects on CCDs. All claims in these patents were used to form the text to be processed by data crystallization and eventually obtain the event map by using KeyGraph.

The graph-based discussion, which took place for 2 h, included one sales manager, two sales engineers, and one regular engineer. They were instructed to talk to each other while looking at the graph output by KeyGraph and told that each opinion should be geared to a scenario for developing products. At first, only one engineer understood the meaning of all the clusters in the diagram and could create scenarios for each cluster. As a group, it was not possible to communicate new words corresponding to the hidden events nor to create new scenarios. We interviewed all the participants after this preliminary stage and found the following two problems:

1. Too many hidden events had to be considered. It was difficult to think of suitable words for expressing hidden events underlying clusters.
2. The word structures were very complex, reflecting the complexity of patent documents, which are composed of purposes, implementations, technologies, etc.

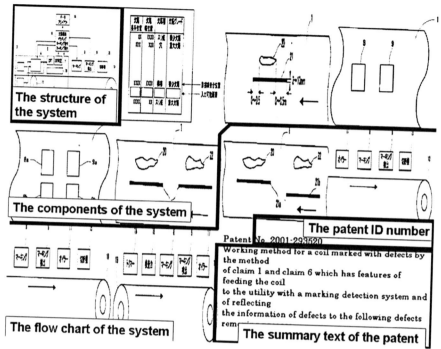

The structure of the system

The patent ID number

The components of the system

The flow chart of the system

Patent No. 2001-293520
Working method for a coil marked with defects by the method
of claim 1 and claim 6 which has features of feeding the coil
to the utility with a marking detection system and of reflecting
the information of defects to the following defects rem

The summary text of the patent

Fig. 3.12 A sample of a pictogram (a visual summary of a patent)

In response to these problems, we introduced the following improvements:

Impr. 1. Choose a few specific patent claim topics so as to focus on limited terminologies.

Impr. 2. Mark each island (cluster) manually with a keyword summarizing the cluster.

Impr. 3. Make pictograms (Fig. 3.12) for all patents. The pictograms, which were visual summaries of each patent, were composed of the patent ID, the flow chart of the patented system, and drawings of the components. When a participant was interested in a certain part of the graph, the corresponding pictograms were collected and pasted onto that part, as in Fig. 3.13. This helped solve ambiguities related to words and concepts.

We incorporated these improvements into the following six-step process and then applied the process to a set of 106 Japanese patents, including both "marking systems" and "inspection," for 2 h with five participants: the four listed above plus an additional engineer. Because four of them had taken part in the preliminary stages mentioned above, we considered this stage the DH process.

Phase 1: Presenting the scenario map

(1) View the graph visualized by KeyGraph with data crystallization. The graph included text data obtained from the documents of 106 patents.

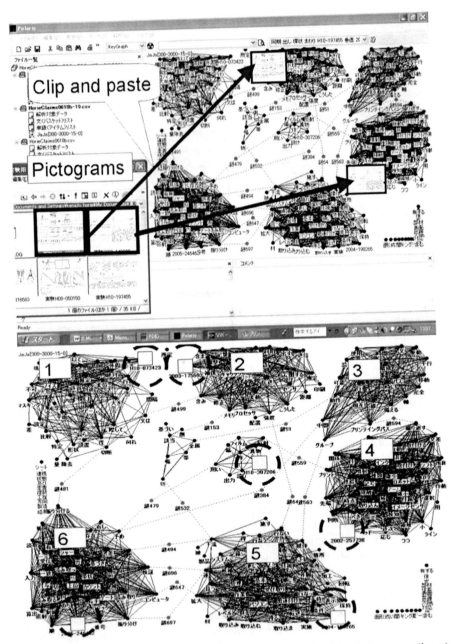

Fig. 3.13 Pasting pictograms on graph (*upper*), and clusters with pasted pictograms (*lower*), obtained in step (4)

Table 3.3 Cluster title and scenarios

Cluster	Item	Scenarios
1	Title	Structure of the marking system
	Scenario	Removes specific defects from unmasked planate area by irradiating laser beam
2	Title	Control of the marking device
	Scenario	Transmits the position of defects on the film by measuring the distance between two defects
	Correction of scenario	Transmits the positional information to the back-end equipment, which then identifies the position of defects
3	Title	Efficiency of the marking system
	Scenario	Moves in parallel with the travel direction of film on a roll and is able to mark multiple defects
4	Title	Ink jet technologies
	Scenario	Robotic arms move marking ink-jet heads automatically to the position of defects
5	Title	Post processing (technology for back-end inspection system)
	Scenario	Compute to detect the position of defects and separate controversial defects to aid visual inspection at back-end
6	Title	Image processing
	Scenario	Allocates a number to each defect on the film
	Correction of scenario	Compute to assign products in allocated gates by reading number issued by image sensor

Phase 2: Discussing the islands

(2) Interpret the events in each cluster and write a title corresponding to the meaning of each (Table 3.3).

(3) Discuss scenarios using the words in each cluster and write them on the white board (Table 3.3).

(4) Find the pictogram corresponding to the technological concept represented by the words in each cluster, as depicted by dotted circles in Fig. 3.13, and reinterpret the cluster while referring to the pictogram.

Phase 3: Discussing the bridges

(5) Paste pictograms corresponding to dummy nodes in the graph by considering hidden events, e.g., "Hidden event 1," to connect the clusters in the graph (Fig. 3.14). Then, write the new scenarios on the white board. For example, the participants created the scenario "change the speed of the CCD conveyer carrying the film on the belt-this might enable back-end checking" by combining cluster No. 5 ("post processing") and cluster No. 6 ("image processing") via the four nodes in the region of "Hidden event 1."

(6) Select new scenarios that all participants agree on and evaluate them from the viewpoint of feasibility of development, marketing, and product novelty.

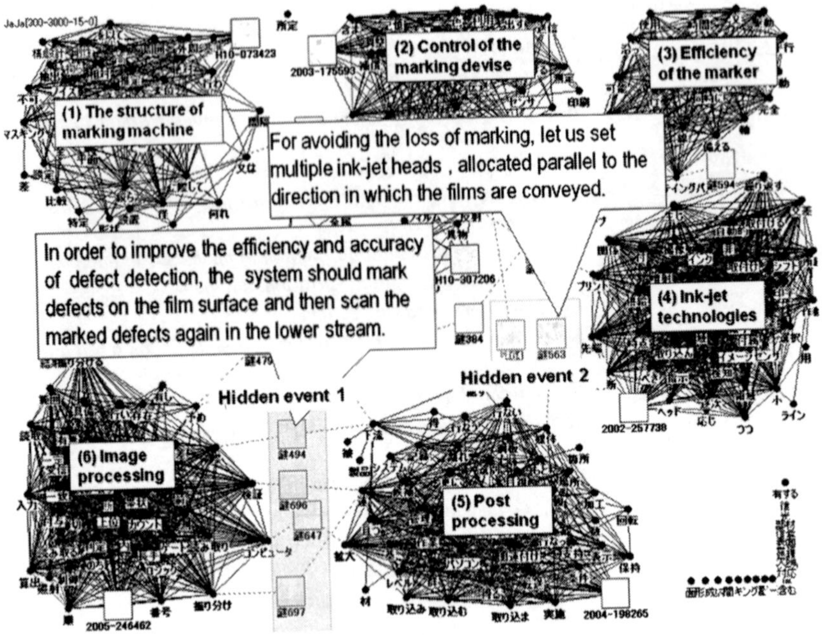

Fig. 3.14 Pasting pictograms on hidden events (steps (5) and (6))

3.9 Results of Data Crystallization for the Development of SIS

We evaluated the effectiveness of the KeyGraph/data crystallization method using the following criteria. (Note: the purpose of this evaluation was to see if the proposed method could enable users to obtain novel and acceptable results for their actual business tasks rather than for our scientific experiments. This is why we do not include a comparison of KeyGraph with other methods but rather check if the externalized hidden events actually contributed to creating useful scenarios.)

1. *Creativity in reinterpreting clusters and correcting scenarios*. Each scenario was meticulously reinterpreted with pictograms for each cluster in step (4). For example, the two scenarios for clusters No. 2 and 6 were corrected by referring to pictograms (Table 3.3). According to the participants, the drawings and charts in each pictogram aided in reinterpreting the cluster. This is similar to the effect of using actual pieces of textile in the previous case.
2. *Creating new scenarios via bridging dummy nodes*. New scenarios emerged from the six clusters by referring to the pictograms of hidden event numbers on the event map in step (5). All five participants paid attention to “Hidden event 1,” which connected the No. 5 and 6 clusters to create a new scenario:

In order to improve the efficiency and accuracy of defect detection, the system should mark defects on the film surface and then scan the marked defects again in the lower stream.

The participants then focused on "Hidden event 2" following the same procedures to propose another scenario:

In order to avoid the loss of marking, let us set multiple ink-jet heads and allocate them parallel to the direction in which the films are conveyed.

New scenarios continuously emerged in this manner, and these scenarios corresponded to the combination of scenarios underlying multiple clusters being bridged by the "hidden events." According to the participants, the hidden events could be interpreted explicitly by talking about both the KeyGraph (based on data crystallization) and the pictograms while being conscious of the process from steps (1)–(6). Finally, five scenarios were proposed for the bridges in Fig. 3.14, of which a random two were selected and are currently being introduced into the development of their new products.

3.10   Summary of the Patent Data Case

In summary, we separated 106 patents into six clusters that clearly had hidden structures and gave them conceptual titles. It was difficult for the participants to think of scenarios that were suitable for redesigning their products because only the top 300 nodal words appeared over excessive links in clusters. We therefore introduced data crystallization and a pictogram for each patent number, which helped the participants to not only interpret each cluster more deeply but also to engage in cross-disciplinary communication creativity (as predicted in the literature on group sensemaking mentioned in Chap. 2). All six clusters were reinterpreted and the initial two scenarios were corrected (Table 3.3).

Furthermore, after the reinterpretation of each cluster, when the participants had moved on to creating new scenarios, the pictograms on hidden events concretized their innovative thoughts and discussion, which, you will recall, had been born of the ambiguity in the information caused by the dummy nodes and clarified by the data crystallization. That is, the difficulty of answering the question "What do these dummies mean?" motivated the participants to perceive useful pieces of information by bridging basic clusters via their interpretation of dummy nodes on the additional information in the pasted pictograms.

3.11   The Process of Interactions for the Spiral of Value Sensing

As we modeled in the double helix (DH) of Fig. 3.1, the real process of chance discovery started with the *collection of data* based on an individual's own or a group's shared business concern. Next, the user(s) introduced the *visualization of data* using suitable tools, which in this case happened to be KeyGraph. They regarded the visualized diagram as a map of the market and discussed scenarios for developing and selling products. Through this discussion, the marketers and designers obtained novel scenarios that they were able to successfully apply to their business. However, we should note that the participants dealt with the mixture of data in real-time as it was collected and visualized rather than refreshing the visualized information as stipulated by the DH model. In other words, participants were faced with a shower of information, and the only successful ones were those who chose what to use adaptively.

After reflecting on the two cases in this chapter, we remodeled the process, as shown in Fig. 3.15, to give the readers a more precise picture of the steps involved. In each case, object data from the real world and subject data from the ideas of the participants, who were the creators of scenarios, were immediately visualized on the white board. This meant that they were always aware of their own current and previous interests and focus points and understood which targets were linked to the core interests of their teammates and how the links might be turned into real benefits in the future. We have been calling this process of chance discovery "double helix" because the individuals and the computer run up a spiral: the individuals give data to the computer and the computer gives visualized results to the individuals. However, after reviewing five successful cases that the participants allowed us to

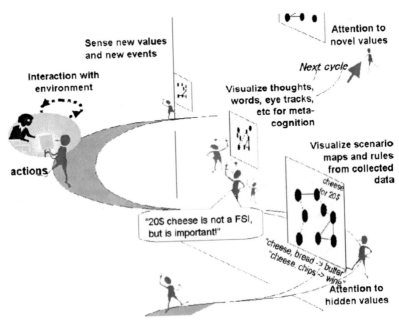

Fig. 3.15 The white board model: The spiral process for chance discovery. Data as objective evidence are the result of subjective interests, and vice versa. Data on both are visualized to the user(s)

publish (of the 38 in our confidential list of application cases as of 2009), we have renamed it the *white board process*. Participants in four of the five cases referred to multiple result visualizations (the output KeyGraph graph for the business data, plus ideas written on the white board or diagrams obtained by applying KeyGraph to the communication text) at the same time, so this new name feels more accurate. Interestingly, among five cases that ended in failure - that is, where no meaningful niche was detected – the users of three of the cases had looked at only the single KeyGraph graph.

In the Innovators' Market Game, the core component of the Innovators' Marketplace – the process of innovation presented in this book –, graphs are visualized for object data and subject data (words representing the participants' ideas) are shown simultaneously by putting the latter on the former. The content of this book reflects the lessons we have learned from our successes and failures in cases we applied to real businesses.

References

Evans J (1987) Bias in human, reasoning: causes and consequences. Erlbaum, Hillsdale

Fine C (1998) Clockspeed. Linda Michaels, Lakeville

Greenacre MJ (1993) Correspondence analysis in practice. Academic Press, London

Han J, Kamber M (2001) Data mining concept and techniques. Academic Press, London

Horie K, Ohsawa Y (2006) Product designed on scenario maps using pictorial KeyGraph. WSEAS Trans Inf Sci Appl 3(7):1324–1331.

Joshi MV (2002) On evaluating performance of classifiers for rare classes. ICDM 2002, Maebashi City, pp 641–644

Lance GN, Williams WT (1967) A general theory of classificatory sorting strategies, I. Hierarchical systems. Comput J 9:373–380

Matsuo Y, Ohsawa Y (2002) Finding the meaning of clusters. In: AAAI fall symposium on chance discovery technical report FS-02-01. AAAI Press, California, pp 7–13

Ohsawa Y (2003a) Modeling the process of chance discovery. In: Ohsawa Y, McBurney P (eds) Chance discovery. Springer, Berlin, pp 2–15

Ohsawa Y (2003b) KeyGraph: visualized structure among event clusters. In: Ohsawa Y, McBurney P (eds) Chance discovery. Springer, Berlin, pp 262–275

Ohsawa Y, Fukuda H (2002) Chance discovery by stimulated group of people, an application to understanding rare consumption of food. J Conting Crisis Manag 10(3):129–138

Ohsawa Y, McBurney P (eds) (2003) Chance discovery. Springer, Berlin/New York

Quinlan JR (1993) C4.5 Programs for machine learning. Kaufmann, San Mateo

Roussopoulos N, Kelley S, Vincent F (1995) Nearest neighbor queries. In: Proceedings of the 1995 ACM-SIGMOD international conference on management of Data, San Jose, 1995, pp 71–79

Soukup T (2002) Visual data mining: techniques and tools for data – visualization and mining. Wiley, New York

Sumi Y, Mase K (2003) Enhancing daily conversations. In: Ohsawa Y, McBurney P (eds) Chance discovery. Springer, Berlin, pp 305–323

von Hippel E (2006) Democratizing innovation. MIT Press, Cambridge

Weiss GM, Hirsh H (1998) Learning to predict rare events in event sequences. In: Proceedings of international conference KDD'98. AAAI Press, California, pp 359–363

Chapter 4
Theories for Innovative Thought and Communication

4.1 Conditions for Creative Cognition

Creativity and innovation represented by invention and discovery are symbols of knowledge-based interactions between human beings. Human creativity has been studied using various approaches: the anagogic approach (Reichardt 1969), the educational approach (de Bono 1971; Gordon 1961), the psychoanalytic approach (Sternberg 1999), the computational psychology approach (Torance 1974), the social science approach (Simonton 1997), the congregative, developmental psychology, artificial intelligence, and cognitive approaches (Runco 1997), design science (Gero and Maher 1993), case studies, and practices (Ghiselin 1952; Wallance and Howard 1989). Of these, the cognitive approach is most useful for revealing the creative process in the human mind – that underlies all thought and communication related to innovation. Experimental methods based on the paradigm of cognitive psychology and observational methods like participant observation have been used to study the process of human creativity in detail.

Some of the most influential research in cognitive science is the creative cognition approach proposed by Finke, Ward, and Smith (1992). They highlighted five research areas in human creativity based on the cognitive approach: (1) creative visualization, (2) creative invention, (3) concept synthesis, (4) structural imagination, and (5) insight, fixation, and incubation. Let us take a moment to discuss each one.

(1) Creative visualization. Finke performed an experiment in which participants designed new patterns by synthesizing/transforming basic figures (like circles and tetragons) and marks (like numbers and alphabet characters), which he called "pre-inventive structures." Participants were asked to predict what their final products would be before and during the synthesizing/transforming process. However, it was quite difficult for them to do so as they progressed through the creative process. This indicates that original ideas evolve during the mental synthesizing/transforming process and that the moment of creation comes as a jumping moment rather than after a long process of logical computing/inferring.

Y. Ohsawa and Y. Nishihara, *Innovators' Marketplace*, Understanding Innovation,
DOI 10.1007/978-3-642-25480-2_4, © Springer-Verlag Berlin Heidelberg 2012

Note that "visualization" here refers to the human act of creating new shapes and visualizing them to others, not the computer-based data visualization we mentioned in Chap. 3.

(2) Creative invention. Finke performed another experiment in which participants tried to create new inventions such as household products and toys by combining basic 3D figures (spheres, cubes, etc.) in their minds. Each participant was given constraints on their creations. The different constraints resulted in different forms of creativity: e.g., one participant would invent a piece of furniture while another would invent a toy. Most of the participants who were given constraints about parts, categories, and functions ("something to carry water in," etc.) made innovative products. In contrast, those who were given constraints about type ("chair," "desk," "bag," etc.), usually failed to make innovative products. Appropriate constraints seem to be key in the creation of innovative products.

Creative invention is of special importance, so we would like to discuss it a little further here. There are two significant findings in Finke's study that relate to our conception of the Innovators' Marketplace. The first is that a constraint on the number of pre-inventive structures encourages, rather than hinders, the creation of meaningful new ideas and products. This may sound counterintuitive to those who believe that the more freedom there is, the greater the creativity, but it makes sense if we provide a constrained set of "basic cards" as the building blocks for creating new products and services. The second significant finding is that pre-inventive structures should be created by the inventors themselves if they want to be the ones creating the new and meaningful ideas.

(3) Concept synthesis. Finke performed yet another experiment in which each participant used two conceptual words and combined them to form a new concept. He found that if a participant used an incongruous combination (such as "enemy" and "bread" rather than "enemy" and "war" or "bread" and "butter"), he/she was more likely to obtain an innovative new concept. Moreover, if a participant was given a category constraint (i.e., the created concept must be in a certain category), he/she could obtain a more innovative concept at higher rate. These results indicate that incongruous combinations are connected to original innovations.

(4) Structural imagination. Ward performed an experiment in which participants tried to imagine and create new objects that do not currently exist but that have features relevant to currently existing types of items, without explicitly mentioning the existing categories. The point was to determine how known knowledge – i.e., existing features – impacts the imagination. The results showed that the objects the participants generated were strongly impacted by the known existing categories that were imagined by the participant from the instructions. This indicates that common knowledge can actually prevent people from creating innovative products. However, innovation is not merely the creation of new ideas but rather of ideas giving novel satisfaction to potential consumers. Therefore, by taking advantage of common knowledge related to

human lifestyles, we can expect participants' thoughts to sync up with their actual living situations and thus create ideas.

(5) Insight, fixation, and incubation. Smith studied the relationship between pre-given knowledge/instructions and generated ideas and found that people were constrained heavily on the knowledge and instructions before the idea genera-tion. This indicates that an individual's own knowledge and ideas under a given context have a strong impact on the generation of new ideas. While this may hamper novelty, it may also urge people to think innovatively – i.e., to create new and market-oriented ideas – if we give them information with a context that is relevant to the desired market.

The results of most interest to us in the above experiments were the use of constraints when creating new products. At a glance, constraints seem to impede creativity, but if appropriate constraints are given, innovative new products can be obtained. Finke has proposed a cognitive model of creativity that includes constraints, and in our research, we have also adopted constraints in the creation of innovative products.

The model proposed by Finke, called the Geneplore model, is a general cognitive model of human creative activity based on the above experimental results. The Geneplore model has two components. First, it represents the human creative process with two steps in the human mind: generating mental images and inter-preting the generated images. When generating mental images, people retrieve their memories and synthesize/transform them to make abstract images that become the cores of ideas. When interpreting generated images, they do so conceptually and determine the function of these images and finally obtain new ideas. These two steps cultivate and improve people's ideas. Second, the Geneplore model includes constraints on the creation of new ideas. Finke has illustrated six constraints on generated products: (1) type, (2) category, (3) function, (4) components, (5) features, and (6) resources.

We used the above findings on cognitive creativity and Finke's Geneplore model to focus on the following three conditions for innovative communication.

- Condition I: The representation of one's own basic concepts, which are the building blocks for creating something valuable, should come from the creator's own mind. These basic concepts should be constrained with a pre-given candidate set. The preparatory basic ideas for innovation, therefore, should be constrained by a limited candidate set, and represented by oneself (or by a group of collaborators). This condition is related to (2) creative invention and also to the first step of the Geneplore model.
- Condition II: Reasoning with combinations and analogy. This is the combination of basic, existing ideas (or technologies) with the analogical transplantation of basic ideas to a new application domain, normally by changing minor parts, so that the basis (a problem for which the basic ideas worked previously) and the target (the present problem in the new application domain) have a similarity. This condition is related to all five of the studies mentioned above. In particular, it refers to our sudden awareness of the similarity between a current and previous

situation in daily life, which is sometimes similar to serendipity when such an awareness results in an invention. This suddenness, which is touched on in both (1) and (5) above, is a driving force behind the two steps in the Geneplore model: in the first, people retrieve imaginary memories from their past to form an analogical solution to a present problem, and in the second, they interpret generated images to solve that problem as well as any problems they created by generating the new images.

- Condition III: Communication while focusing and shifting contexts. Participants should be encouraged to discuss each other's contexts and ideas from the viewpoint of heterogeneity, working through conflicts to reach a suitable consensus. This condition, which is related to (1)–(5) above, is also a driving force behind the Geneplore model: in the first step, individuals share each other's images through compassion and empathy (see Sect. 4.2), so that the mental image can be reformed to fit their own problem solving in their own contexts, and in the second step, they interpret either the shared images or the images they created on their own after reformation. Criticism and evaluations of an individual's idea further refines the second step. We will discuss this in more detail later, but briefly, constructive criticism and questions by highly trained staff enable individuals to externalize the potential problems of proposed ideas and replaces the act of *doing*, which is an essential step in the process of reaching a group consensus about the products or services to be designed. Ideally, the ideas are improved via the interaction of participants in a discussion. In this interaction, ideas diverge via context shifting and converge via focusing, as required in Lindberg et al. (2010). This enables all kinds of the constraints we have mentioned to be externalized and reflected upon in order to think up, reject, and improve new ideas. This can be difficult in that participants might give up if they think they are alone in their opinion about something, or the discussion in general might take on a depressing air. We feel that this difficulty can be eased somewhat by using a game for the discussion.

The remainder of this chapter is divided into three parts corresponding to these three conditions. In the first part (Sect. 4.2), we present a basic model for knowledge externalization by representing one's own basic ideas (Condition I). We focus in particular on the effect of metacognition. In Sect. 4.3, we deal with methods for reasoning with combinations and analogies (Condition II). In Sect. 4.4, we deal with methods for communication by focusing on and shifting contexts (Condition III). We discuss the effects of question-asking and criticism here. We summarize the chapter in Sect. 4.5.

4.2 Process for Innovation and Representing One's Own Basic Ideas

Representing one's own basic ideas is a key component of externalization in the SECI model, which is the most widely used process for knowledge management (Nonaka 1994). The SECI model, shown in Fig. 4.1, is used to explain the process of

Fig. 4.1 Flowchart of SECI model

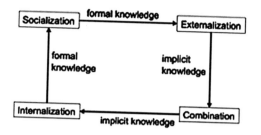

creating, sharing, and using systematic knowledge within a company. In this model, there are two types of knowledge: tacit knowledge and formal knowledge. Tacit knowledge is based on experiences and guesses and tends to be difficult to represent in spoken or written words. In contrast, formal knowledge can be explained and represented by texts, images, equations, etc. As the SECI model unfolds, tacit and formal knowledge are transformed and relocated among individuals, groups, and the organization as a whole. To put it simply, SECI can be regarded as a process of transforming and relocating different types of knowledge. The continual transformation of knowledge enables a company to sustain its creativity.

The SECI process has four phases: socialization, externalization, combination, and internalization. In the socialization phase, tacit knowledge is obtained and transmitted by sharing the experiences of members in the same workplace. In the externalization phase, the obtained tacit knowledge is transformed into formal knowledge by talking and writing and then shared among colleagues. In the combination phase, new formal knowledge is created by combining the acquired formal knowledge obtained in the externalization phase. Finally, in the internalization phase, the new formal knowledge, which has evolved, is shared throughout the workplace and the process can begin again with the next socialization.

It is worth pointing out that all knowledge is generated from an individual's experience, including their interactions with customers in the market. In this sense, SECI is not only a model of idea creation but also of innovation in that it can improve the market showing as well as a company's performance. In order to boost mutual understanding within a group, people exchange their implicit knowledge (this corresponds to the socialization phase), but it is difficult to share tacit knowledge with others. To solve this problem, most people transform their tacit knowledge into formal knowledge by using text, images, equations, etc. (this corresponds to the externalization phase). Thus, verbalized formal knowledge is more concrete than tacit knowledge. We expect this transformation to accelerate people's understanding of the essence of knowledge. In other words, the metacognitive effect we mentioned earlier is caused by verbalization, so the participants notice significant latent factors relevant to their own business performance. Acquired formal knowledge is used as material for creating new systematical and comprehensive knowledge (this corresponds to the combination phase). IT tools such as groupware and other knowledge-based systems, which may include functions to visualize data, can be useful in this process. When people get stimulated by knowledge originating in other sections, new knowledge is created. The development of new products by combining all the separate small ideas corresponds to the combination phase. Systematical and comprehensive knowledge can be obtained in the form of a document or manual to help people apply new knowledge to their tasks. These people need to absorb new types of knowledge, i.e., knowledge they can put into immediate action, through their own experiences (this corresponds to the internalization phase). The newly acquired implicit knowledge can then be shared with others through the socialization phase. The SECI model assumes that this process will continue for a long time in what is known as a knowledge creation spiral.

4.2.1 Externalization of Basic Ideas by Owners

In the SECI model, externalization means to share created knowledge within a group. Therefore, it is important for SECI users to present their acquired knowledge in basic terms so that other members can easily understand in order to ensure smooth new steps of knowledge creation. However, basic ideas written or spoken in easy words by one person are usually too abstract to use or to combine with other ideas. Thus, users are encouraged to express basic ideas (based on their tacit knowledge) along with some additional information (like the touchable materials and pictograms we described in Chap. 3). This accelerates empathetic, compassionate communication and enables participants to compensate for missing information caused by the hidden constrains and intentions behind the basic ideas.

Furthermore, if a basic idea in one's brain is externalized for others, they can use it as the seed of new idea that can solve a problem. Any new idea made from unknown basic ideas, or from ideas made by some unknown person, will not be useful in terms of solving problems (as we mentioned with respect to pre-inventive structures), so externalization is always necessary. This process should be done in accordance with a form or other system co-ordinated by the users themselves.

There are many methods that can be used to externalize ideas. The simplest are verbal and manual: people mentally translate their own basic ideas into new information that can be understood by others, and then they either speak it aloud or write it down. This translation makes basic ideas more accessible. This is similar to the phase of generating mental images in the Geneplore model. The externalization of basic ideas by speaking obviously requires listeners, and if there are none, recording tools like voice recorders should be used so that the spoken information can be shared later. Externalizing ideas by writing, in contrast, requires neither listeners nor recording tools. Writing a diary entry is a good example. Other examples include Weblogs and other social media such as My Space, Facebook, and Twitter and recently Google+. People do not need to write perfect sentences: they can simply note basic ideas.

After information about a basic idea has been verbalized, some people may require additional information in order to understand it if the words and sentences in these tentative sentences are inadequate. In such cases, annotating the sentences is a good way to add information that may correspond to hidden intentions or constraints relevant to the context. Annotations can include lines under certain letters, circles around certain words, symbols to mark certain words and sentences, and so on, and additional sentences can be added near the underlined ones. Recently, with the increased usage of digital documents, there has been increased development of software for making annotations, which is often available for free.

Writing information and understanding/interpreting the underlying semantic structure is one verbalization technique that accelerates the effect of metacognition. For example, Tony Buzan developed the Mindmap (an example is shown in Fig. 4.2) as a tool for creativity support (Buzan and Buzan 1995). This is a map showing the relationships between different pieces of information that the user has added, as well as words and additional lines/curves connecting the words. User make and revise the map by organizing the complex information structure to solve the given problem.

First, the main problem is drawn at the center of the Mindmap. If this problem is quite big, sub-problems relating to it are also drawn. Problems are connected with solid lines if they are related to each other. Information relevant to each problem is also drawn and connected where necessary. The completed Mindmap shows users which information can be used, which has been missed, and which should be discarded.

Although there are many methods for externalization, it is generally known as a quite difficult phase. For example, *how-to* manuals are not always easy for customers to use. Customers tend to complain that these manuals lack required information. One reason they may be poorly organized is that the technical experts involved with the development of both the products and the manuals are not always skilled at externalizing tacit knowledge. That is, how-to manuals are written by technical experts who have a lot of tacit, up-to-date knowledge on the product – including the constraints that should be considered to take full advantage of the product features – and such experts often do not externalize their tacit

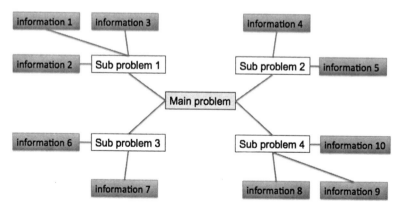

Fig. 4.2 An example of a Mindmap. The main problem to be solved is drawn in the center. Sub-problems and related information are drawn around the main problem. Related problems and information are connected with solid lines (or *curves*)

knowledge because they can already use their products without really being aware of constraints. Essentially, they are too close to their own work.

Although there are plenty of tools to externalize ideas and knowledge, people have to exchange externalized information with their colleagues in order to recognize the missing information – that is the difference between tacit and formal (externalized) knowledge. As a solution to this problem, we propose that the obtained implicit knowledge is transformed into formal knowledge by the receiver of the knowledge rather than the giver. If the receiver becomes aware of something missing in the proposed or explained knowledge, he or she can add it by re-externalization. Our main point here is that, although it is important to run long-term cycles of the four phases in the SECI model, we also need to run shorter-term cycles in the externalization phase.

4.2.2 Metacognition

After people have obtained represented information about basic ideas, they have to look at this information and reflect upon it. This action, called metacognition, is the self-recognition one's own cognition. Metacognition as a technical term was first coined by Flavell and Brown in the educational psychology and developmental psychology field (Brown 1987; Flavell 1987). In the academic field, it has been used to interpret the development process of a child's learning ability. Metacognition can be trained a posterior. In this sense, because value-sensing is an acquired trait in humans and sensemaking is strongly linked with value sensing (see Chap. 2), metacognition is an essential factor in the cognitive functions that rule the process of sensing valuable ideas from interacting with the market and of creating scenarios for innovation by taking advantage of those ideas.

For a long time, metacognition has been used as a factor in the interpretation of the development process of a child's learning ability. In this book, we take metacognition to mean an action for innovative thought. For example, let us take coffee as a basic idea. Many people drink several cups of coffee per day, but they may have different reasons for performing this same action that depend on individual situations and contexts. If people in an office drink coffee, it may be that they would like to quench their thirst or to stay awake while completing repetitive tasks. These reasons are quite common. On the other hand, if people outside an office drink coffee, it may be that they would like a moment to relax and take a rest, or just to pass the time. If we asked people from this second group why they drink coffee, they might say, "I like to drink coffee when I have nothing special to do and just want to pass the time, because … so … the aroma of coffee makes my brain active, and … reminds me of things I have to do. Right, that's it. I walk out of the office when I feel I've forgotten something important, and having a cup of coffee helps me concentrate." In this case, metacognition gives us new information about the role a cup of coffee and provides a new idea: to construct an office-work environment where staff can perk up and complete assignments on schedule.

The metacognition of, say, individuals in Japan who buy 100 yen cups of coffee from McDonald's could also be useful. If they say, "I don't like coffee so much, but 100 yen is pretty cheap, and all I want to do is relax after walking around the city," the McDonald's staff could try to promote such behavior by providing comfortable spaces to take a rest.

As we tried to show in the above examples, metacognition is useful not only for clarifying information that is not clear but also for discovering new information that can lead to the creation of new ideas. Therefore, we encourage people who are trying to achieve innovation to tap into their metacognition by representing thoughts about basic ideas. Just start writing or speaking, and one word will call up other words from your tacit knowledge and deepen the level of externalization.

4.3   Reasoning with Combinations and Analogy

As stated before, humans represent information about their own basic ideas by verbalization and metacognition. The next step is figuring out how to apply these basic ideas to target problems. In this section, we discuss the effects of combinations and analogy for reasoning.

4.3.1   Reasoning with Combinations

If you want to create a new idea, what should you think about? We all know it seems difficult, or even unrealistic, to think up ideas that have never existed before. Let us look at some of the ideas thought up by past inventors. Specifically, how and about what did they think?

Masayoshi Son is the man who came to be the founder and president of Softbank Inc., a mobile phone company in Japan. In his younger years, he strengthened his own idea-making ability by a method he invented himself. He prepared cards on which the names of household goods were written. Then, he chose two cards randomly, looked at them, and created a new idea by combining the two goods. It is important to stress that he always used both household goods to think up the new idea. He could think up innovative ideas from combinations of households that, when taken individually, did not seem to have much potential for success.

A number of innovative things – such as NASA's space shuttle and Apple Inc.'s iPad – have been created by combining more than two things that already exist. We call this method for idea creation *combinatorial thinking*. The Innovators' Market Game that we introduce later features a communication space in which participants practice combinatorial thinking to obtain business ideas.

Combinatorial thinking has long been used for making new ideas, as noted by experts in a number of fields as well as by researchers on the science of creativity (Mahmoud-Jouini and Charue-Duboc 2008). Combining existing basic ideas to create new value is a standard approach to creation. For example, the saws and hammers used by carpenters were invented by combining existing items such as helves (for grip) and metallic materials (for cutting and striking). More recently, commercial items have been created by combining a brand name with an existing item. Manufacturers of famous brands tend to be attracted to this type of creation, which they build on the fame of their own brands. For example, Apple Inc. invented a new jogging kit that is a combination of their own iPod and NIKE Inc.'s Airwalk shoes. The jogging kit records the length of the run and the amount of burned calories. Although this combination did not require a technical investment, the kit has been bought by a large number consumers because it appeals to older consumers as well as the young. The brand recognition of Apple and NIKE, which make this a very visible product, and the fact that the kits provide a new jogging style for experienced joggers as well as beginners, has resulted in very high sales for this product. It seems clear that these details were direct results of combinatorial thinking.

Here, we should note that in order to achieve innovation, one should choose suitable items to combine: combining a random set of items simply will not work. For example, take the iPad, which has a simplicity that attracts users. If the iPad had come with a fixed physical keyboard on its face, it would probably not have become such a successful product. Data mining methods can aid people in choosing the best things to combine by providing a list of recommended items (Kurz and Stoffel 2002; Nishihara et al. 2007); even so, it is the individuals themselves who must ultimately decide which things to choose. What is the best way for them to do this? We present one solution in the following sections.

4.3.2   Reasoning with Analogy

As most people know, it is difficult to solve a problem if we start with insufficient information. Ideally we apply solutions, with or without modifications, that have been used for previous problems. We call this technique analogical thinking. To put it simply, analogical thinking is when an individual takes advantage of the similarity between two problems, or objects representing the problems, to solving the current problem. For example, if a person finds a similarity between problem A and problem B, he or she can solve problem B, called the target, by remembering the solution to problem A, called the base. Analogical thinking is a metacognitive activity of remembering, modifying, and applying previous solutions for the base to solving a target problem that is similar to the base. Analogical thinking supports all kinds of cognitive activities involved in problem solving, including reasoning, explaining, creating, etc.

The process of analogy has four steps. Let us look at a mathematical problem as an example. As stated, people often start by recollecting a previous problem and then attempting to solve the target problem by applying the solution of the previous problem, with modifications if necessary. They also evaluate how appropriate the correlation is, i.e., if the new (target) problem has a similar structure to the previous (basic) problem or if the similarity is just superficial. If they decide that the correlation is both sufficient and structural, they solve the problem and also save the solution as knowledge that can be used for similar problems in the future.

The above is an example of the four steps of analogy. In the first step, one mentally recollects experiences (bases) that are similar to the target. When looking for bases, not only superficial but also structural similarity is important. In the second step, one connects the details of both problems by comparing the base with the target. Knowledge for solving the target problem is obtained by mapping from a base problem. In the third step, one evaluates the degree of correlation (i.e., the similarity). Analogy is flexible in that it can come into effect even if there is only a partial correlation between the base and target problems, but there is a risk of misguided attempts at solving the target. Structural similarity with sufficient granularity is necessary to avoid such missteps. In the fourth step, the solution is filed away for future use with new problems. The experience of solving the target problem by using the base problem(s) are stored as abstract knowledge that includes the relationship, patterns, and rules between the two problems. Overall, analogy can be regarded as a reasoning process that can expand and reconstruct knowledge.

Many innovative products have been created by using analogical thinking. One example is the mechanism of helicopters. This might be a little difficult to picture, so let us introduce the target problem: How does a helicopter fly forward when an airscrew is whirling round and round? To solve this problem, let us consider a Japanese flying toy for children called a bamboo-copter (Fig. 4.3). This toy flies forward when thrown at a tilt. How does a bamboo-copter fly? This is a good base for solving the target above, because a simple experiment with a bamboo-copter will show that the airflow around the rotating screw pushes the toy forward. As for finding the similarity between the bamboo-copter and a helicopter, we find that both have a shaft in the center, vertical to the earth, and that an airscrew whirls around the shaft. These points, linked with airflow dynamics, demonstrate that the two objects

Fig. 4.3 A bamboo-copter, a Japanese toy

share a structural similarity. We can thus infer that a helicopter flies forward if its airscrew is whirled at a tilt, similar to a bamboo-copter.

Let us look at two types of research relevant to the link between analogy and combination. The first type has relied on descriptive evidence from cognitive psychology literature showing that the same individual can describe different meanings to a given word in different contexts, thereby producing new interpretations (Gentner and Markman 1997). Such ambiguous interpretation involves a contextual shift in one's own mind, often called subjective transfer (Waldron 1979). These ideas can be applied to the design of the helicopter in that we notice the possibility of interpreting the flight of a bamboo-copter from various aspects – it flew due to the lightweight nature of its material and also due to the screw. Obviously we cannot connect the bamboo-copter's material (bamboo) to the helicopter, but we can apply the screw and its tilt, which may match that of the aircraft body. In other words, we focus on just one of several aspects of the solution of a memorized problem and then apply our interpretation to the current problem, thus combining the borrowed idea with features of the current problem. This is the key concept of analogical reasoning: the cross-domain transfer from the base (events, items, words, etc. given in advance) to the target (the current event, where the human problem-solver may require concepts emerging from the base). Analogical reasoning has been essential in the creation of concepts (Gomes et al. 2006; Holyoak and Thagard 1995) and has been elucidated by structure mapping theory (Gentner and Markman 1997; Gentner et al. 1993), which enables the transfer of basic knowledge to different domains where other pieces of knowledge are waiting to be combined. These studies can be useful in business once we detect a source of ambiguity, i.e., words/items/events that may result in multiple interpretations. The second type of research has focused on detection and interpretation performed via interactions with colleagues and with the market. For example, in chance discovery (Ohsawa and McBurney 2003; Ohsawa and Tsumoto 2005), events in which the future is uncertain have been explored to enable novel, effective decision making. Chance discovery provides profits to business executives because the graphs visualized by chance discovery methods supply hints for linking past and current events – which can be rare and ambiguous and sometimes difficult to notice – to multiple events and scenarios. By noticing such events, users can externalize new problems they should solve and thereby determine which new decisions they should make.

4.4   Communication Methods with Focusing and Shifting Contexts

People can use information about basic ideas to make new ideas by combinatorial thinking and analogy. The next step is communicating about their new ideas with focusing and shifting contexts. In this section, we discuss communication methods in which ideas are improved and new ideas are obtained. It is best if the key step of *doing* (testing) is included in the process of developing innovative products and services, as emphasized in Skogstad and Leifer (2010). We recommend users introduce the doing step during, rather than after, this communication phase because it plays an essential role in stakeholders reaching a consensus inside and even outside of a group of collaborating members. Consensus here includes the satisfaction of customers after a product or service has been launched in the market. However, long-term services and strategic visions are difficult to test. In such cases, communication between highly trained staff that includes questions and constructive criticism enables potential problems and infeasible use-situations to be externalized. This takes the place of the doing step.

4.4.1 The Role of Questions and Constructive Criticism

If people come up with new ideas by combinatorial thinking and analogical thinking, they should explain clearly what the value of new idea is so that it can be properly applied to new products/services. If they cannot explain the value, the idea obviously cannot be diffused into society as a valuable one. One of the most important factors when explaining the value of a new idea is considering the viewpoints and opinions of others, but these can often be difficult to determine. In such a case, one possible solution is to obtain them from other people directly.

Ideally, the person who came up with the idea should ask others what they feel the disadvantages of the idea are. These disadvantages will then have to be improved. Therefore, it is desirable to obtain as many different viewpoints and opinions as possible.

Merely listening to others talk about the disadvantages is not an effective way to obtain meaningful information. Of greater value is question asking and constructive criticism. These two are similar in that the question "Does the tool you invented work well in such a case?" can potentially be considered a criticism: "Your tool does not work well in such a case." If the problems highlighted by such questions and criticisms are resolved, the value of the original idea may increase because the different contexts of the participants motivates each to view the idea from new points of view.

In the field of industrial design, Eris suggested that successful designs are the result of good questions (Eris 2004). When he noticed the importance of asking questions, Eris videotaped a design project graduate students in engineering design were performing for 2 weeks. He found that certain questions had a significant effect on pivotal decisions, and that the questions and obtained decisions appeared to be closely linked. In order to analyze the relationships between question asking and decision making, Eris selected five previously published taxonomies from four different research areas: philosophy, education, artificial intelligence, and cognitive psychology.

The first was made by Dillon (1984), who undertook 12 categories of questions for the research areas of education, philosophy, psychology, and history. However, he found that there were not any taxonomies commonly available for all areas. If detailed analysis was needed, specific taxonomies had to be made.

The second one, made by Aristotle and presented in the textbook "Posterior Analytics," was comprised of four categories of questions: existence (affirmation), nature (essence/definition), fact (attribute/description), and reason (cause/explanation). This taxonomy focused on distinguishing different types of questions in accordance with the level of an individual's knowledge. The third one, for the research area of artificial intelligence, was made by Lehnert (1978). She proposed the theoretical foundation of a computational model for answering questions. In her model, the question answering process is divided into two categories: understanding questions and finding answers. To develop the latter part of the model, she made 13 categories of questions. The fourth one, for the research areas of cognition and education, was made by Grasser (Grasser and McMahen 1993). Grasser used Lehnert's taxonomy and added five more categories of questions. He used his taxonomy to analyze the frequency and the type of questions asked by students. He found that certain questions - found in the goal orientation, causal antecedent, causal consequent, expectational, procedural, and enablement categories – were correlated positively with a student's learning. He termed such questions "Deep Reasoning Questions (DRQ)." Most of the taxonomies by these four researchers have many categories in common.

In order to determine the specific categories of questions in industrial design, Eris analyzed three videotape recordings of communication in which design ideas were created by students. Questions defined as verbal utterances related to the design tasks at hand that demanded explicit verbal and/or nonverbal responses were extracted and tagged with the categories of questions published in previous research. Although most of questions were tagged as deep reasoning questions, 15.4% of them were not. These questions were related to divergent thinking, which is necessary for generating new industrial designs (whereas Deep Reasoning Questions might be intended to encourage convergent thinking). Such questions were termed "Generative Design Questions (GDQ)" and divided into five categories: proposal/negotiation, scenario creation, ideation, method generation, and enablement. What this means is that humans need both convergent and divergent thinking to create valuable ideas. Thus, people involved in industrial design are encouraged to engage in both convergent and divergent discussion. This demonstrates how controlling the question asking can aid people in creating innovative designs and ideas.

How can we control question asking? There has been one method for this proposed in the field of requirement engineering (Kushiro and Ohsawa 2006), which is a type of engineering used when formulating the process of requested specifications for software, services, and products. Software needs to be developed according to the clients' specifications, but of course, not all clients are skilled at phrasing their requests in a precise way. In order to avoid complaints from clients, developers have to know the exact specifications, and if they ask the right kind of questions, they can obtain the required information. Kushiro and Ohsawa's method focused on obtaining the customer requirements that were most important in the early stages of product development. Prior conditions and constraints for requirements were also obtained by using this method. The key feature of the method is semi-structured interviews in which interviewers ask questions about the purpose, requirements, and techniques related to new products of both the consumers and the developers. The questions they ask have two aspects: positive and negative. The interview process is as follows.

(1) If a customer mentions a new requirement, the interviewer asks clients for both positive and negative reasons about the purpose, i.e., what is the purpose he/she advocates the requirement and what happens if he/she gives up the purpose, in order to position the requirement with linking to the latent intention.
(2) Next, the interviewer asks clients for positive and negative reasons about the requirement itself, i.e., why the requirement is essential for the purpose in (1) and why that requirement may be meaningless for the purpose, in order to reveal alternative requirements.
(3) Finally, the interviewer asks about specific techniques to fulfill the requirement, mainly to developers. When answers are obtained, the interviewer asks for both positive and negative comments about the ideas.

Interviewers do not need any special training or skills to ask these questions. The method itself is related to previous methods for externalizing tacit knowledge: laddering (Corbridge et al. 1994) (which is also an interview method) and claim analysis (Carrol 2000). In laddering, human requirements are represented as a hierarchy, and interviewers ask customers over and over again why they must have these requirements in order to grasp the essential point of their requirements. In claim analysis, the benefits and defects of a design are drawn up in order to determine the constraints necessary to make the design possible and to define how to satisfy the clients' demands. Kushiro and Ohsawa combined these methods to create a new one that can reveal customer requirements and represent these requirements as a structured, high-quality knowledge set.

When asking negative questions, people need to sympathize with other's ideas if they intend to obtain good ideas. Even when they receive a negative response to an idea, sympathy is required so that all participants can develop feelings of empathy for each other. This will enable them to feel the underlying context of each idea (or question or criticism) so that they can revise their ideas (or questions, etc.) to fit each others' contexts – that is, they can improve their ideas. We cannot stress enough that a game – like atmosphere is essential for participants to remain in a positive mood when they are surrounded by questions and criticism that may be negative.

4.4.2 Using Personas to Make Scenarios for Diffusing Ideas

In the old days, most commercial items and products were so simple that people could use them without any instructions. Nowadays, however, many items and products are painstakingly designed for individual customers, and because they can be quite complicated, developers need to have a clear idea of what the individual's desires are. The persona method is useful for drawing up an imaginary outline of the mind of an individual consumer (Cooper 1999). The word "persona" has the same origin as "personality," and the word "character" has a similar meaning: i.e., a human's natural features. Personality indicates a mask, i.e., a character with a social standard. Persona also indicates an imagined aggregation of individuals, rather than a single specific individual, who are the target of developers' innovation. Developers set personas to specifically focus on the key targets in their market. In other words, they use imagination and a consideration of user benefits and merits to develop commercial items and products.

In order to set personas, product/service developers must first clarify who the targets are and what natures they have. They do not need to clear them up quantitatively. In most cases, qualitative data are used for setting the personas in this first step. For example, a persona is set by using the imagination:

A boy. His name is John and he's in the 5th grade of elementary school. His hobby is watching the night sky with a telescope. He would like to be an astronaut in the future.

Making personas enables the developers to discuss the scenarios more smoothly, because focusing on individuals makes it easier to think about the details. In addition, the way the discussion is set up enables people to choose how they diffuse new commercial items and products. Here, note that focusing on a certain context of a persona is a subjective activity for the developers. This subjectivity may be met with some resistance by developers who prefer objective and reproductive activities, but the subjective approach is actually quite beneficial because the creation of successful products and services always requires some information about future situations in which the products and services will be used - in other words, scenarios that do not appear as objective facts in the data about the past. Thus, people seeking innovation in their business should make several scenarios for a new idea by utilizing the subjective imaginations and emotional utterances of all participants. This enables simple scenarios to evolve into more developed ones.

4.5 Summary

In this chapter, we introduced three conditions for innovative communication as well as methods for satisfying them. The relationship between the two is shown in Table 4.1 and an example of the actual process is shown in Fig. 4.4. We gave examples of new ideas created under these conditions, but in a real-life situation, we cannot always follow this ideal process. One lesson we learned from a large number of cases in real workplaces was that these conditions do not necessarily appear in a fixed order: e.g., we might start with satisfying Conditions II and III if the situation forces us to. In some cases, we may have to be flexible and skip Condition II. The point is to keep an eye on all three conditions all the way through the never-ending process of innovation.

Table 4.1 Relationships between the three conditions and methods for satisfying them

	Condition I: Representing one's own basic concepts	Condition II: Reasoning with combinations and analogy	Condition III: Communication while focusing and shifting contexts
Externalization	Y		
Metacognition	Y		
Combination		Y	
Analogy		Y	
Question-asking			Y
Criticism			Y
Persona			Y

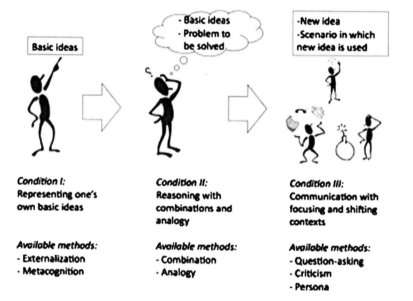

Fig. 4.4 Process of innovative thought driven by the three conditions

References

Brown AL (1987) Metacognition executive control, self-regulation and other more mysterious mechanisms. In: Weinert FE, Kluwe RH (eds) Metacognition, motivation, and understanding. Lawrence Erlbaum Associates, Hillsdale

Buzan T, Buzan B (1995) The mind map book. BBC Books, London

Carrol JM (2000) Making use: scenario-based design of human-Computer interactions. The MIT Press, Cambridge

Cooper A (1999) The inmates are running the Asylum. Sams Publishing, Indianapolis

Corbridge C, Rugg G, Major NP, Shadbolt NR, Burton AM (1994) Laddering: technique and tool use in knowledge acquisition. Knowl Acquis 6–3:315–341

de Bono E (1971) New think: the use of lateral thinking in the generation of new ideas. Basic books, New York

Dillon TJ (1984) The classification of research questions. Rev Educ Res 54:327–361

Eris O (2004) Effective inquiry for innovative engineering design. Kluwer Academic Publishers, Boston

Finke RA, Ward TB, Smith SM (1992) Creative cognition: theory, research, and applications. The MIT Press, Cambridge

Flavell JH (1987) Speculations about the nature and development of metacognition. In: Weinert FE, Kluwe RH (eds) Metacognition, motivation, and understanding. Lawrence Erlbaum Associates, Hillsdale

Gentner D, Markman AB (1997) Structure mapping in analogy and similarity. Am Psychol 42:45–56

Gentner D, Rattermann MJ, Forbus KD (1993) The roles of similarity in transfer: separating retrievability for inferential soundness. Cogn Psychol 25:524–575

Gero JS, Maher ML (1993) Modeling creativity and knowledge-based creative design. Lawrence Eribaum Associates, Hillsdale

Ghiselin B (1952) The creative process. University of California Press, Berkley

Gordon W (1961) Synetics: the development of creative capacity. Harper & Row, New York

Grasser A, McMahen C (1993) Anomalous information triggers questions when adults solve quantitative problems and comprehend stories. J Educ Psychol 85(1):136–151

Gomes P, Seco N, Pereira FC, Paiva P, Carreiro P, Ferreira JL, Bento C (2006) The importance of retrieval in creative design analogies. Knowl Based Syst 19:480–488

Holyoak KJ, Thagard PR (1995) Mental leaps: analogy in creative thought. MIT, Cambridge

Kurz T, Stoffel K (2002) Going beyond Stemming: creating concept signatures of complex medical terms. Knowl Based Syst 15(5–6):309–313

Kushiro N, Ohsawa Y (2006) A requirement acquisition process as an evolved chance discovery, chance discoveries in real world decision making. Springer, Berlin, pp 315–328

Lehnert GW (1978) The process of question answering. Lawrence Erlbaum Associates, Hillsdale

Lindberg T, Meinel C, Wanger R (2010) Design thiking: a fruitful concept for IT development? In: Plattner H, Meinel C, Leifer L (eds) Design thinking: understand – improve – apply. Springer-Verlag, Heidelberg, pp 3–18

Mahmoud-Jouini SB, Charue-Duboc F (2008) Enhancing discontinuous innovation through knowledge combination: the case of an exploratory unit within an established automotive firm. Creat Innov Manag 17/2:127–135

Nishihara Y, Sunayama W, Yachida M (2007) Creative activity support by discovering effective combinations. Syst Comput Jpn 38(12):99–111. Wiley

Nonaka I (1994) A dynamic theory of organizational knowledge creation. Organ Sci 5(1):14–37

Ohsawa Y, McBurney P (2003) Chance discovery. Springer-Verlag, Berlin Heidelberg New York

Ohsawa Y, Tsumoto S (2005) Chance discoveries in real world decision making. Springer-Verlag, Heidelberg

Reichardt J (1969) Cybernetic serendipity: the computer and the arts. Praeger, New York

Runco MA (1997) The creativity research handbook. Hampton Press, Cresskill

Sternberg RJ (1999) Handbook of creativity. Cambridge University Press, Cambridge

Simonton DK (1997) Historiometric studies of creative genius. In: Runco MA (ed) The creativity research handbook. Hampton Press, Cresskill, pp 3–28

Skogstad P, Leifer L (2010) A unified innovation process model for engineering designers and managers. In: Plattner H, Meinel C, Leifer L (eds) Design thinking: understand – improve – apply. Springer-Verlag, Heidelberg, pp 19–43

Torance E (1974) Torrance test of creative thinking. Scholastic Testing Service, Bensenville

Waldron RA (1979) Sense and sense development. Andre Deutsch Ltd., London

Wallance D, Howard EG (1989) Creative people of work: twelve cognitive case studies. Oxford University Press, New York

Chapter 5
Analogy Game: Training and Activating Analogical Thought

As we mentioned in Chap. 1, innovation, which is more than the mere creation of novel ideas, can be achieved in an environment where suitable constraints are placed on human thought rather than allowing people to freely speak out ideas. We developed a Web-based environment for a word categorization exercise called the Analogy Game (AG). This game aims to elevate the inherent ability of individuals to externalize concepts based on existing words. In AG, players are engaged in analogical reasoning that contributes to the integration of words and leads to the construction of new concepts. We tested AG using both experienced employees working at companies and junior high school students. Both groups were presented with ambiguous words and asked to categorize them. Our results suggest that the presentation of ambiguous stimuli is associated with the analogical process of innovative thought. The older players, who have long been engaged in innovative work both at school and in their companies, tended to apply more insight to the word categorization, whereas the younger players relied more on trial and error. We present this case along with a case in which artists improved their work (based on their own evaluation) after playing AG. These cases show how AG works to measure and elevate innovative thought.

5.1 Introduction

Analogy, as we discussed in Chap. 4, is a cognitive process of transferring information from a particular subject (the base) to another (the target). Analogical reasoning is useful if we know what the base domain is and what the relationships between the base and the target domains are – in other words, the similarity between the past and present situations. For example, the similarity between the flight of a bamboo-copter and the expected flight of a helicopter is that they fly and sometimes hover at the same location. Designers can use their awareness of this similarity to borrow the idea from the bamboo-copter and apply it to the helicopter to control the tilt angle

Y. Ohsawa and Y. Nishihara, *Innovators' Marketplace*, Understanding Innovation,
DOI 10.1007/978-3-642-25480-2_5, © Springer-Verlag Berlin Heidelberg 2012

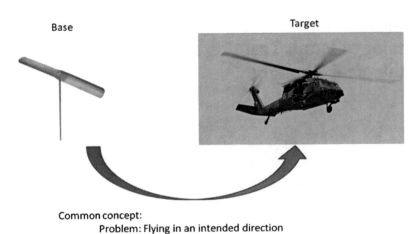

Fig. 5.1 Analogy via similarity (common concept) between base and target

of the screw. As illustrated by this example, noticing a similarity means finding a concept common to multiple items (Fig. 5.1).

This awareness of common concepts, which is the core idea of analogy, can be achieved by simple manipulations of everyday words. We know that combining a common keyword with a word that is becoming increasingly popular tends to result in hit products (Nishihara et al. 2007). Similarly, the Q-methodology (Brown 1996) uses the human manipulation of word-cards to reveal subjective structures, attitudes, and perspectives. In our Analogy Game (AG Nakamura and Ohsawa 2008a, b), which we introduce in this chapter, players (users in a relaxed emotional state) arrange and rearrange a limited number of word-cards on a desktop. Each player *must* create five or less groups of words, without leaving a single word uncategorized, which results in concepts that correspond to all the created groups. The extent of the change from the initial arrangement of word/phrases-cards is evaluated as the game score – which, incidentally, is only given to encourage players to be earnest in their manipulation of the word/phrase positions. It should be noted that the players' behavior, not their score, is what is important for training and elevating their use of analogical thought. AG is our attempt to strengthen analogical thinking by providing the opportunity to use ambiguous words or phrases as hints that stimulate "sleeping dragons," in our original wording. In other words, to externalize latent problems and relevant concepts that may improve business performances via inventing new designs of products/arts/services (Gick and Holyoak 1980).

AG can be used as a method for reinforcing the computer-aided discovery of useful concepts, as in (Nishihara et al. 2007), where rewards and constraints are given to the user (player). We can also look at AG as a tool for obtaining useful scenarios and concepts or for observing human cognitive behavior in the process of creating and externalizing concepts. AG players explore their thought processes while creating scenarios that are both new and meaningful for the market they are engaged in. Computers do not interpret any of the human conceptualization; they merely supply players with an environment in which they can continuously think.

5.2 The Outline of Analogy Game

First, players are presented with word/phrases-cards on a screen (Fig. 5.2) and instructed to rearrange them into groups corresponding to appropriate higher-order concepts. The players color-code, name, and provide written descriptions of the concepts underlying each cluster. They continue to restructure the clusters with coloring words in each cluster by the same color, constructing new concepts, until all items have been placed into a conceptual category.

Most of the words (both words and phrases are put words hereafter) in AG are simple nouns because we expected them to elicit ambiguous perceptions from the players that would evoke analogical thinking in the process of combining words into concepts. However, we sometimes use technical terms related to a certain domain so that players who are experts of that domain can externalize latent concepts and problems.

The process of rearranging the cards is shown in Fig. 5.2a–c. Each player is given a limited number (normally 20) of words/items, each of which appear in a small square node. Initially, the words are placed randomly (Fig. 5.2a: the words in the initial state may be categorized randomly by the host machine). As players rearrange the cards, they can write their interpreted meanings of the words in balloons (Fig. 5.2b) via the interface. By the end of play, all the ambiguous items must belong (i.e., be color-coded) to one of the groups created by the player (Fig. 5.2c).

We prepared a word-card set of 20 words (including "bottle cap," "baseball," "Internet," etc.), that could be adapted for different experiments. The system architecture consisted of a network environment with a browser for players to access the system. This browser also kept logs of all the user interactions.

5.3 The Model of Concept Creation as the Basis of AG

Our model of the process of concept creation is shown in Fig. 5.3. Players try to categorize words by relating a group to episodes in their real or imagined experiences and ultimately obtain a fully categorized state, where each word belongs to one group. Working with the established principle that external information and constraints motivate (rather than impede) creativity (Bonnardel 2000; Finke 1995; Hori 2000), we instructed the players to categorize all word-cards into five groups or less without leaving any word uncategorized, as mentioned earlier. In order to

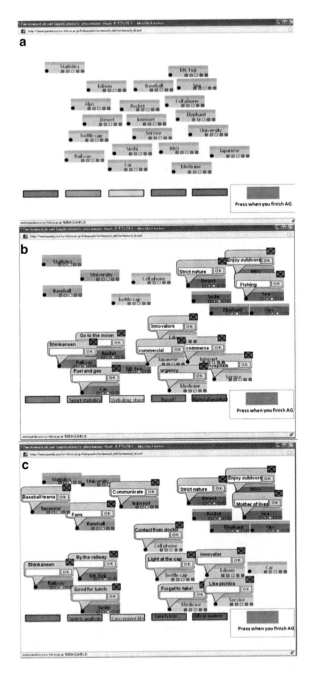

Fig. 5.2 A sequence of snapshots during Analogy Game (AG) play, from initial state (**a**) to ending state (**c**). (**a**) Words/phrases are randomly positioned. (**b**) Two phrases, "cell phone" and "bottle cap," are isolated. (**c**) Clusters are reconstructed and new concepts appear

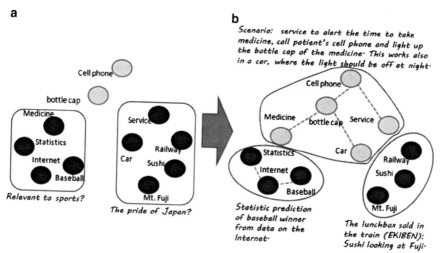

Fig. 5.3 The process of word categorization as analogical thinking. (**a**) Some words remain uncategorized. (**b**) All words have been categorized, with relating each category to a concept. Some concepts can be interpreted as scenarios, i.e., stories about events/items represented by cards

deal with this constraint, players have to construct, destruct, and reconstruct groups during play. By reflecting on realistic episodes from daily life and matching them with words on the display, some of the obtained groups become linked to imaginable or feasible scenarios.

We hypothesized that players would first address items that looked easy to categorize and then address the more difficult ones afterward. By giving the constraint that all items must be categorized, we expected that the pressure to reconstruct clusters, as depicted in Fig. 5.1, would encourage insight (Mayer 1992). That is, an impasse, in which a player desires to move beyond prefabricated ideas and to construct new concepts, thereby complying with the instruction to place each item in a category, acts as pressure to overcome the impasse (Shank 1982). Insight, by which we mean the introduction of a useful variable to explain the observation of being released from the impasse, should facilitate the categorization of all words. Without insight, players would rely on trial and error to fit any remaining items into a cluster. In this regard, we presumed that older players would tend to have greater insight because their more extensive life experience enables them to understand concepts both explicitly and implicitly with greater ease.

5.4   Experiment (I): Comparison of Older and Younger Players

5.4.1   Experimental Method

All words in AG were simple nouns with ambiguous meanings (e.g., "Lincoln," which could be construed to mean a U.S. president, the name of a place, or the name of an automobile). Twelve participants including business people who had worked for companies for more than 5 years (older players), and twenty junior high school students (younger players) participated in this experimental AG. Each player was given 20 words. At the start, the words were randomly placed, as in Fig. 5.2a.

We performed two trials of the experiment with no break in between. The first trial included no special instructions, while in the second one, players were instructed to focus on a given social issue (e.g., ecological issues). The reason we gave this instruction is that the effect of analogical thinking tends to be reinforced with an explicit focus of context/topic toward a target (Finke 1995; Gick and Holyoak 1980). We chose social issues because mental processes reflect social processes (Mead 1934) and because insights depend heavily on social interactions (Csikszentmihalyi and Sawyer 1995).

5.4.2   Results: Analogical Thought and Experiences

We analyzed the data obtained from the gaming logs as follows. First, among the three types of recorded actions involved in the procedure (dragging items, coloring items, and providing written descriptions of the meanings of items), two formed the core of our analysis owing to their direct relation to conceptualization (coloring and providing meanings). Second, we defined the ambiguous items to be extracted from the 20 word-cards. Third, on the basis of the time-series data of the actions, we compared the group of players. We used the following definitions for our analyses.

5.4.2.1   Clusters and Their Meaning

Color-coding was regarded as the core action of the cognitive process underlying the construction of concepts reflected in the grouped word clusters. The awareness of a group, called a cluster, was defined by Eq. (5.1), where the experimental time was normalized by 50 as $t = \{0, 1, 2, \ldots, 50\}$, i.e., any time length of a one-trial game by a player was scaled to 50, with 0 as the start time and 50 as the end of the game. Here, the number of actions required to color card C_i is defined as $g_i(t)$, and G denotes the total number of actions in one game.

$$G = \sum_{i=1}^{20} \sum_{t=1}^{50} g_i(t) \tag{5.1}$$

The cognition reflecting the awareness of meaning was captured in the same manner as the cognition reflecting the awareness of clusters. It was defined by Eq. (5.2), where the number of actions required to fill in the blank (see Fig. 5.2) with the written meaning of an interpretation is expressed as $h_i(t)$.

$$H = \sum_{i=1}^{20}\sum_{t=1}^{50} h_i(t) \qquad (5.2)$$

5.4.2.2   Definition of Ambiguous Items

Uncategorized words, regarded as the result of an impasse, were deemed "ambiguous" and were extracted in the following manner. We defined a set of word-cards as $\{C_1, C_2, \ldots, C_{20}\}$. The time d required for G', which means the rate of cards remaining uncategorized, to attain 10% in Eq. (5.3) is represented by t.

$$G' = \sum_{i=1}^{20}\sum_{t=1}^{50} g_i(t)/G \qquad (5.3)$$

This equation is for identifying those word-cards that were left until the end of the experiment (i.e., the last 10% of all actions).

The moment (one unit in the normalized time) at which a great number of coloring actions occurs can be regarded as when strategies enabled a progression toward the formation of concepts insofar as concept recognition involved several word-cards. In contrast, if the pace fades, it means that progress has halted for some reason, such as being engaged in some other manipulation or involved in a deep thought. The manipulation hypothesis should be discarded because the interface is so simple that, according to player interviews so far, players can both write the meanings of words and color/move them at every minute of the game.

Thus, we denote the time at which the greatest number of coloring actions, i.e., the actions to create or restructure clusters, occurred before t^d by t^m and call it the *cliff*, meaning the situation just before falling down to the valley of vacillation. The time gap between the mode (t^m) and the time coming close to the final coloring action (t^d), where the length of vacillation is defined as $t^d - t^m$ if larger than 0 and as 0 otherwise. This length is 49 at maximum ($t^m = 1$, $t^d = 50$). We associate the longer vacillation durations with more deliberate explorations of strategies and insights for coping with ambiguity and the shorter durations with smooth interweaving of thought and actions.

In the first trial, we tried to extract ambiguous items from both the younger and older players in accordance with the method outlined above. With the younger players, the procedure revealed 11 players with ambiguous items and 8 players without. Here, we considered a vacillation lasting longer than 10 s to indicate the presence of ambiguous items. We used Eqs. (5.1) and (5.2) to compare the processes of these players. Figure 5.4a–d shows the polynomial-function approximation of the 10th order.

5.4.2.3 Younger Players

Figure 5.4a shows that the color-coding of items to form clusters increased prior to the task of providing written descriptions of meaning (before t^m). After this, the entries of word meaning continued at a fast pace, whereas clustering activity slowed down. In other words, around the middle of the game (between t^m and t^d), players tended to color a few items but leave others uncolored, i.e., ambiguous items not belonging to any cluster. At this stage, they began to write word meanings while considering how to integrate or explore common concepts among the uncolored cards. They sometimes externalized a new concept by rearranging a set of cards and redefining their meaning (by filling in the blanks) so as to accommodate the previously uncolored cards. In the "valley of vacillation" between t^m and t^d, players confirmed that ambiguity led to the acquisition of new concepts, according to their

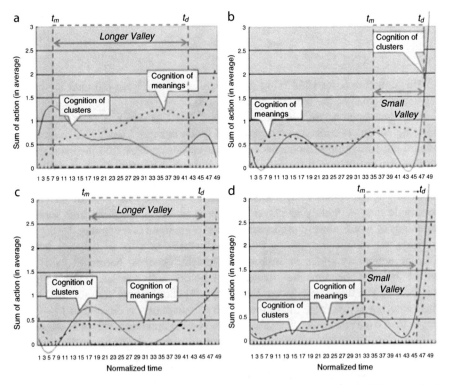

Fig. 5.4 The valley of "sleeping dragons," meaning the period between t^d and t^m in normalized time. The length of the valley was, for younger players, (**a**) more than 10 (in normalized time unit: 50 units correspond to the full time of one game for each player) when encountering ambiguous items (8 players) and (**b**) less than 10 when no ambiguous items were encountered (12 players). For the older players, the length was (**c**) more than 10 when encountering ambiguous items (8 players) and (**d**) less than 10 when no ambiguous items were encountered (4 players)

comments after the experiments. Finally, they colored and moved words reflecting the obtained concepts (after t^d).

Players who reported no ambiguous items, on the other hand, demonstrated two processes (see Fig. 5.4b): (1) actions that altered colors when writing the word meanings, which appeared as valleys shorter than the typical valleys of vacillation in cases of the type in Fig. 5.4a, and (2) coloring actions that greatly increased the pace during the final stage after t^d. This implies that smooth interweaving of shallow thought and quick actions of clustering lasted from the beginning to the successful end, as evidenced by the smaller valleys that often appeared in the early stage of the procedure.

In either case for younger players, the valleys varied in size (see the "valleys" in Fig. 5.4a, b) and represented an important feature of vacillation due to ambiguous words. That is, a long-lasting valley indicates that an insightful thought for solving an ambiguity is taking place. This implies that a long vacillation contributes to the externalization of latent concepts.

5.4.2.4 Older Players

Next, we present the process of the older players. We performed the same analysis as above and found that four players had ambiguous items and eight did not. Figure 5.4c, d show the process underlying the clustering and meaning-making. The form of the graphs shows a significant difference between ambiguous items and no ambiguous items, similar to the case of the younger players, which supports the idea that ambiguous stimuli affect the thought process in concept creation (Nakamura and Ohsawa 2008).

5.4.2.5 Comparison of Younger and Older Players

Here, we focus on our analysis of the difference between the thought processes of younger and older players who either did or did not encounter ambiguous items. Older players with ambiguous items tended to have valleys that were smaller that those of the younger players (Fig. 5.4a, c). Note that these graphs represent the average of eight players for each of (a) and (c). We can interpret this to imply that younger players require more time and actions (*trial & error*) than the older ones to activate analogical thinking for concept externalization when stimulated with ambiguity.

In contrast to the existence of several valleys in the case of younger players without ambiguous items (Fig. 5.4b), we find only one small valley in the case of older players with no ambiguous items, as shown in Fig. 5.4d. Furthermore, the color-coding of items was concurrently synchronized with the meaning assignment for the entire period of time to play: even the one small valley was nowhere close to being a valley of vacillation. This non-existence of major valleys implies that older players, who have more experience with life events, simultaneously consider

Table 5.1 The independent evaluation of externalized concepts

Younger players		Novelty	Interestingness	Utility
With ambiguous words	Average	13.3	10.6	6.8
	Std. variation	5.3	3.6	4.7
Without ambiguous words	Average	8.4	6.8	6.6
	Std. variation	4.2	3.8	4.5
Older players				
With ambiguous words	Average	13.9	11.5	11.4
	Std. variation	4.1	4.0	4.0
Without ambiguous words	Average	7.3	4.5	5.8
	Std. variation	2.4	2.9	3.6

both clustering and word meaning; that is, people with more experience tend to feel less ambiguity when categorizing everyday words and can easily choose concepts corresponding to presented words on the basis of their experience.

5.4.2.6   Evaluation of the Externalized Concepts

After the concepts that had been externalized in AG by all the players were shuffled, the list of concepts was evaluated by five business people. These five were selected because we felt they could evaluate ideas from the viewpoint of practical application to the real world. Such a viewpoint is essential to determine if an externalization is a useless idea or a creative one that may be relevant to innovation linked to a social contribution. The evaluation was done by ranking each concept from lowest (1) to highest (5).

The results of the evaluation are shown in Table 5.1. We found significant differences between the cases with and without ambiguity, especially in terms of novelty and interestingness. We evaluated the significance of the differences by t-testing and certified the differences, except for practical utility, by the significance level of $p < 0.05$. In the case of business people, this difference was validated by t-test, including for utility. These results demonstrate that dealing with ambiguous words encourages the externalization of useful, novel concepts. This is a significant finding when we consider how difficult it is to promote fundamental creativity in the average workplace, and we expect this "ambiguous information" element of AG to be used as a principle for reinforcing the power of innovative thought.

5.5   Experiment (II): Effect on Artists' Work

In this section we discuss artistic activities, with a particular focus on the identification of the themes of artwork and artistic designs. This is a domain in which limited research has been conducted, although there has been some. For example, comparative analyses between interpretations of literature and design tasks have been discussed (Nagai et al. 2009). With the intent of analyzing artist's thoughts, in this section we analyze the process underlying interpretations of categorized words by replicating the data contained in players' gaming logs. A relevant analytic technique has been introduced in a study that observed artists for more than a year (Okada et al. 2007): a detailed case study of two artists showed that analogical thoughts regarding similarities between current and new themes encouraged creative cognitive process and cultivated higher-order artistic design concepts, which in turn led to novel ideas. Here, we partially borrow ideas from Okada's approach in that we investigate the artistic creative process - not the mere birth of new ideas but rather of something expected to touch a viewer or listener's heart - by which awareness of a novel theme emerges from existing themes.

5.5.1 Experimental Method

Fourteen artists (eleven women and three men), all graduates of the Tokyo University of the Arts, participated as members of one of the following four groups.

- A team: Japanese-style painters (5)
- B team: Sculptor (1) and oil painter (1)
- C team: Masters of wood-engraving (1), wood-carving (1), and oil painting (1)
- D team: Oil painters (4)

Twenty words (nouns) were presented and listed by one representative from each group, who then clustered these listed words into, at most, five groups and named a concept that described each group. The rest of the gaming process was basically the same as in previous sections: after all players were given the word-cards produced by the representative of their group, they each arranged them on a PC screen to reconcile the cards with their own ideas (See Fig. 5.5(1)). Then, the players were asked to reconstruct the clusters by considering the meaning of each word (Fig. 5.5(2)). The time limit, 30 min, was set for all players on the basis of the time required in preliminary experiments.

Players were asked to draw any picture that reflected the ideas of the clustered concepts that emerged from playing the Analogy Game (Fig. 5.5(3)). Only a pencil, an eraser, and a piece of A4-sized paper were used for drawing. The drawing time was limited to 20 min for all players.

Each player was asked to create a title for his/her drawing and to explain the drawing by using the provided words and the name of the cluster created in AG. They were also asked to describe how the new depiction differed from the original.

5.5.2 Experimental Results

When the artists played AG, they wound up creating novel themes in their representations, which shifted from a realistic/impressionistic style to a more abstract

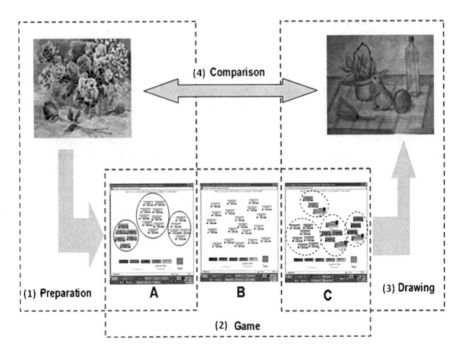

Fig. 5.5 Analogy Game process with artists

and imaginary style – i.e., beyond the realities of space and time. The details of
their cognitive processes were replicated based on the data in the logs and feedback
from the players. Because the strategies used tended to emerge during the game,
the replication divided the procedure into first and second halves, each with two
parts (four steps in total). One case is shown below to provide a visual example, but
similar effects (the influence of words on the artwork created after the game) were
found in all cases. In the following representations, the names of the word groups
are in curly brackets { } and the word-cards are in inequality signs <>.

5.5.2.1 The Case of a Japanese Artist (Player A)

At the beginning (see Fig. 5.6)
{Drawing subjects} = < plant >, < spider >, < Solidago altissima >
{Materials} = < foil >, < rock palette >, < whitewash >
{Reality} = < free task >, < cold >, < diversion >, < oxidation >, and
< black and white >
{Intention} = < respect >, < actuality >, < chill >, < challenge >, < fact >,
< want >, < world >, and < time >
{Exercise} = < unfinished >

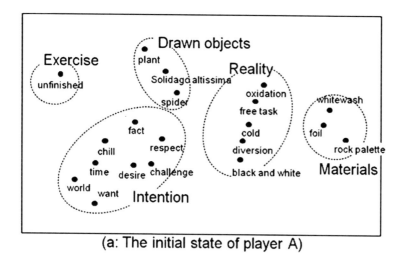

(a: The initial state of player A)

Fig. 5.6 The sequence of actions while a Japanese artist (player A) plays AG: initial state

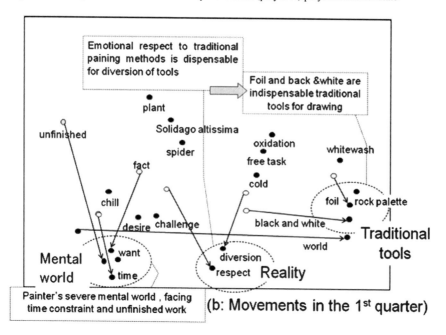

(b: Movements in the 1st quarter)

Fig. 5.7 The sequence of actions while a Japanese artist (player A) plays AG: movements in 1st quarter. Each movement of a word is shown by an *arrow* from a white to a *black dot*

From the beginning through the first quarter (see Fig. 5.7)

Because the cards had been categorized according to whether the words referred to observable ({drawn objects} and {materials}) or to unobservable ({intentions}) phenomena, player A, a Japanese-style painter, consolidated {drawn objects} and {materials} while thinking about the mental <world> of professional Japanese-style painters and considering other words referring to invisible phenomena. Traditional Japanese-style painting utilizes <foil> and <rock palettes>, and it is a {reality} that professional painters are rigid with regard to the <time> needed to complete an <unfinished> piece of work.

The second quarter, to the midpoint (see Fig. 5.8)

Player A was thinking that the <free task> corresponds to the <unfinished> task by virtue of a relationship between opposite concepts. The <world> of player A had been placed in the same group as <unfinished>, but here was moved to the group containing {materials} because her interest moved from the imaginary to the real world.

The third quarter (see Fig. 5.9)

Japanese-style painting is not only hard work; it is also a freely chosen activity in the real <world>. The severe <fact> is the <unfinished> work under the constraint of <time>, which is the <world> of {reality} to player A who is daily working under the hard real constraint of time.

The last quarter, to the end of the game (see Fig. 5.10)

<Unfinished> was categorized into a negative group, whereas <free task>, <desire>, and <wants> were placed in a positive group as motivators for pursuing Japanese-style painting.

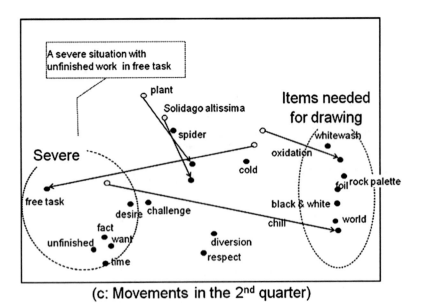

(c: Movements in the 2nd quarter)

Fig. 5.8 The sequence of actions while a Japanese artist (player A) plays AG: Movements in 2nd quarter

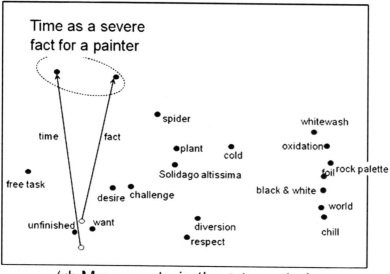

(d: Movements in the 3rd quarter)

Fig. 5.9 The sequence of actions while a Japanese artist (player A) plays AG: Movements in 3rd quarter

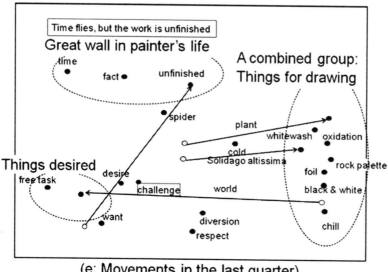

(e: Movements in the last quarter)

Fig. 5.10 The sequence of actions while a Japanese player (player A) plays AG: Movements in final quarter

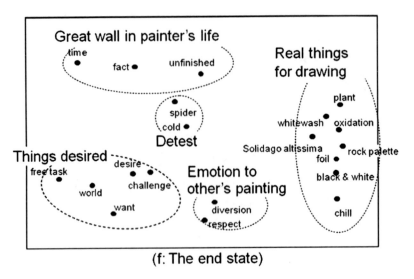

(f: The end state)

Fig. 5.11 The sequence of actions while a Japanese artist (player A) plays AG: End state

At the end of the game (see Fig. 5.11)
{Materials} = <plant>, <Solidago altissima>, <oxidation>, <chalk>, <foil>,
<black and white>, <rock palette>
{Emotional involvement with other paintings} = <diversion>, <respect>
{Detest} = <spider>
{Facing wall} = <time>, <fact>, <unfinished>
{Things one wants to do} = <free task>, <cool>, <desire>, <wants>,
<challenge>, <chill>, <world>

We can compare the processes of this player at the beginning and end of the
Analogy Game by looking at Fig. 5.12. According to player A, the new drawing
really expresses her mental world, where she is challenging the wall of *time*, which
stands for the *fact*, i.e., the most difficult constraint in her life. We find that the
words time and fact were touched in the third quarter, which is when the movement
of word-cards was the lowest. This indicates that the valley of vacillation not only
created a high number of ideas but also had a strong influence on creative activity.

5.6 Discussion

In cases where ambiguous items were presented as basic words, the players were
given a task requiring the creation of concepts. The reconstruction of word groups
in the face of ambiguous words and the constraint forbidding players to leave
any word uncategorized enhanced rather than impeded the concept externalization.

Fig. 5.12 The artworks
before and after AG. (**a**) The
original picture. (**b**) The
drawing after the game

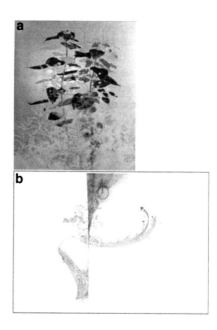

This tendency is evident when we observe that players consider latent contexts in the midst of the thinking process (the *valley of vacillation*) when they assign meanings to words and word groups but do not construct groups – in other words, when they are trying to overcome an impasse. In this regard, the valley of vacillation can be considered a form of Finke's exploratory cognitive process.

In our earlier comparison between players classified by age, the older players, who we assume have been engaged in innovative work in business for some time, tended to gain insight efficiently during word categorization, whereas the younger players relied more on trial and error. Similarly, in cases where an artist improved their performance after playing AG, the concepts obtained in the valley of vacillation can be linked to the artwork produced after the game.

These results demonstrate the effectiveness of using AG to measure, train, and enhance innovative thinking. (Please note, however, that there is another feature of AG that is taken advantage of in the Innovators' Marketplace, which we introduce in Chap. 6). In other words, the side product of AG – the thought that reflects a player's tacit ideas underlying experiences – is used as a resource for producing basic cards. The human ability to use analogical thought can be positioned as the basis of chance discovery and a gateway to value sensing as individuals undergo the following four sub-processes, i.e., sensing, recollection, scenariozation, and co-elevation:

1. Sensing external events. Feel the possibility that an element of real life has the potential to be something new, and be motivated to collect data on events latently relevant to the future life of oneself. For example, the data on exhibited products we mentioned in Chap. 3 may have given hints in the creation of a sellable product. This initial sensing enables people to collect data from the environment.

2. Recollection. Explain situations underlying observed events in the real world. This enables people to collect subject data from fragments of human thought so that the thoughts can be visualized as a list of sentences or as a graph showing the relation among words that describe the thoughts.
3. Scenariozation. Tell stories about the past and invent stories about the future. These stories are presented as a sequence of situations, events, or actions occurring in a coherent context, which is why we call them *scenarios*.
4. Co-elevation of scenarios. Exchange scenarios with colleagues. Scenarios may be combined, as in the cross-over patterns of genes, to make a new scenario that is acceptable to most participants. Participants need to embody a new value criterion that is sharable among colleagues. The cross points of scenarios are identified and presented as a strong candidate for a *chance*.

The whole point of these four processes is for individuals to activate analogical reasoning. The latent value of daily events, i.e., their possibility of being a chance, is sensed in (1) by feeling a similarity between the confronted event and one in the past. The past event functions as a basis and the present event as a target. In the recollection phase (2), utterances by users are the evidence of their analogical reasoning. For example, we came across a marketer who said, "The Indian textile reminded me of a lady wearing a cloth of a similar texture on a hot day in summer," which is an example of how an individual's past experience worked as the basis for solving a target problem, i.e., what the Indian textile means for consumers. In (3), a scenario may emerge from an analogy between a past experience of events and the connection of nodes on the visualized graph. For example, the same marketer said that the corduroy textile in the center of Fig. 3.7 (Chap. 3) could be used as a material for soft suits on the basis of his experience designing a suit (basis) with a fabric that had a smoothness and strength similar to corduroy (target). Another marketer said that corduroy is more useful for a lady's one-piece casual garment on the basis of his experience observing students at a women's university wearing a cloth of similar thickness and color (basis) to the corduroy (target). Finally, phase (4) can be illustrated by the analogical reasoning of the marketer with the most experience, who said, "The desire of business people, who wear suits every day, is to change into something more comfortable on the way home from the workplace. This desire can be satisfied by using corduroy for a semi-business (semi-casual in other words) jacket, which is professional but looks OK after work." This is an example of analogical reasoning used to apply multiple bases (casual cloth possibly made of the corduroy, a semi-business jacket he remembered from the past, etc.) to the target (a discussion about using softer fabric for suits). In other words, he noticed the similarity among three items – what business people desire, what young women want to wear, and what corduroy is like – and externalized the latent value "soft and natural for both work and after" via the communication of multiple marketers with different experiences and viewpoints.

In summary, the key elements are:

- Multiple participants representing stakeholders with different experiences and viewpoints
- Basic knowledge collected from various stakeholders to function as bases in solving new problems
- Each participant's sense of analogy, which can be activated by simple tools such as the Analogy Game
- Hints for linking the bases to the targets, e.g., the graphs obtained by KeyGraph with data crystallization

The findings we outlined in this chapter support us in coordinating a process of innovative communication (such as the Innovators' Marketplace) and provided us with the tools we needed for the Innovators' Market Game introduced in the next chapter.

References

Bonnardel N (2000) Towards understanding and supporting creativity in design: analogies in a constrained cognitive environment. Knowl Based Syst 13:505–513

Brown SR (1996) Q-methodology and qualitative research. Qual Health Res 6:561–567

Csikszentmihalyi M, Sawyer K (1995) Creative insight: the social dimension of a solitary moment. In: Sterngerg RJ, Davidson JE (eds) The nature of insight. MIT Press, Cambridge

Finke RA (1995) Creative insight and pre-inventive forms. In: Sternberg RJ, Davidson JE (eds) The nature of insight. MIT Press, Cambridge

Gick ML, Holyoak KJ (1980) Analogical problem solving. Cogn Psychol 12:306–355

Hori K (2000) An ontology of strategic knowledge: key concepts and applications. Knowl Based Syst 13:369–374

Mayer RE (1992) GESTALT: thinking as restructuring problems. In: Thinking, problem solving, cognition, 2nd edn, Chap. 3. Freeman, New York, 39–78

Mead GH (1934) Mind, self, and society. University of Chicago Press, Chicago

Nagai T, Kayama M, Itoh K (2009) A drawing process model for a drawing-learning support system in the networked environment. In: Proceedings of the 23rd annual conference of the Japanese society for artificial intelligence, Takamatsu, June 2009

Nakamura J, Ohsawa Y (2008) Insight or try & errors: ambiguous items as clue to discovering New Concepts in Constrained Environments. In: Proceedings of knowledge-based intelligent information and engineering systems: KES2008 (LNAI). Springer, Berlin/New York

Nakamura J, Ohsawa Y (2008) Ambiguity Items as Clue to Concept Creation, Introducing an Analogy Board, In: Proceedings of 14th International Conference on Cognitive Science, Seoul

Nishihara Y, Sunayama W, Yachida M (2007) Creative activity support by discovering effective combinations. Syst Comput Jpn 38:99–111

Okada T, Yokochi S, Namba K, Ishibashi K, Ueda K (2007) The interaction between analogical modification and artistic vision in the creation of contemporary arts. Cogn Stud 14(3):303–321

Shank RC (1982) Dynamic memory: a theory of reminding and learning in computers and people. Cambridge University Press, Cambridge

Chapter 6
Innovators' Market Game: Communication with and for Innovative Thinking

In this chapter, we introduce a board game called the Innovators' Market Game (IMG). This game provides players with a communication space for thinking up innovative ideas, which they create by combining existing products, services, business ideas, and so on. They not only obtain new ideas but also evaluate the quality of each idea. Three types of players – *inventors*, *investors*, and *consumers* – discuss whether or not the new ideas are of value in the marketplace. This has typically been considered a difficult task, but in the game, the players find they are enjoying themselves as they work through the processes and eventually create feasible ideas. IMG has already been used by business people, students, researchers, and academic faculty members to produce innovative ideas, some of which are currently in the pre-production stage.

In this chapter, we discuss the following:

- How to communicate among stakeholders to create innovation (Sects. 6.1–6.6)
- How to play the Innovators' Market Game (Sects. 6.7 and 6.8)
- How the game board supports players (Sects. 6.9 and 6.10)

6.1 Communication Between Stakeholders for Innovation

As we have learned from our work with individuals in real businesses, the ideas required for societal change emerge from human communication. As far as we know, ideas that have been embraced in the marketplace have never emerged from just one person's brain: communication and consensus are as important as individual insight. IMG players are therefore encouraged to communicate with the aim of creating and externalizing ideas that sell.

We have also learned of the importance of role-playing: i.e., communication in which participants – including people who invent and provide products/services, those who consume them, and those who invest in them – act out their various roles in the marketplace. Using role-playing in IMG enables players to engage in

Y. Ohsawa and Y. Nishihara, *Innovators' Marketplace*, Understanding Innovation,
DOI 10.1007/978-3-642-25480-2_6, © Springer-Verlag Berlin Heidelberg 2012

communication that both diverges and focuses ideas. The roles correspond to the various stakeholders taking part in the process leading up to innovation. Some of the stakeholders concentrate on thinking up new ideas, while others concentrate on evaluating the ideas.

Role-playing communication between stakeholders is similar to the role-sharing seen between inventors and investors in entrepreneurial ventures in Silicon Valley in the late 1990s. Those inventors were young students who had learned cutting-edge techniques at top universities. They were highly motivated, had time to think and work, and did not have much money. These young students often visited rich investors, called Angels, to make pitches explaining their business plans backed up by new techniques and new ideas. Most of the investors of those days had established their companies after interacting with and learning from the expanding market. They hoped to earn more money by investing in new companies that were part of the expanding marketplace. They surveyed the inventors' plans in detail, held discussions, sometimes gave advice, and often invested money in promising inventors. This culture of playing roles ("inventors" and "investors" in this case) has since spread to other countries.

In IMG, role playing offers two main benefits in terms of realizing innovation. The first is that players can concentrate on their own specific roles. If they had to play several roles, they might get confused, especially if there were time restrictions, as in a board game. The second is that ideas evaluated as suitable by most of the players are eventually deemed the noteworthy ones. In order to make this possible, in IMG, the ideas are evaluated not by the people who came up with them but rather by other players, who select, prune, or improve the ideas as necessary. This separation of proposers (inventors) and evaluators (investors and consumers) enables the most highly evaluated ideas to eventually be chosen. It is for these reasons that the communication between stakeholders playing respective roles is positioned as the key concept of IMG.

6.2 Three Stakeholders: Inventors, Investors, and Consumers

There are three types of stakeholders in IMG: inventors, investors, and consumers. All three are considered innovators because they all contribute to innovation. The role of the inventor is to propose new ideas and the role of the investor is to evaluate the potential of each idea and then invest money in the inventor whose ideas show the most promise. The role of the consumer, of course, is to buy the most appealing ideas (products/services). They are encouraged to criticize the ideas if they see flaws. We proposed the original version of IMG in 2007, and all of the players were inventors. After many trial games, we added investors and consumers because we felt they were also contributors to innovation. In the following sections, we explain how and why we added these new stakeholders in more detail.

6.3   Inventors: The Creators of Ideas

On a stormy evening in December 2007, four members of the laboratory, including the first author (the second author Nishihara joined Innovators Marketplace since 2008), were trying to think of something interesting to do. The author proposed a new and simple game for them to play. In this game, each player should think up new ideas for an interesting business and write the ideas on slips of paper. The players can buy ideas proposed by the others, and they can also combine their own ideas with those they have bought to propose new ideas. The player who has the most money at the end is the winner.

The players seemed to enjoy the game. However, they stopped thinking up new ideas fairly quickly because, to be honest, not many of the ideas seemed very useful for a real business, and they were not exactly selling well. Through additional trials of the game, we noticed that it was necessary for someone to evaluate and critique the proposed ideas – someone coming from a different point of view than the players who proposed the ideas.

6.4   Investors: The Evaluators of Inventors' Talent

After the trials mentioned above, we added the role of investors to the game. The communication between two stakeholders (an inventor and an investor) was expected to be useful for the generation and selection of useful ideas.

The role of investors is to invest money in inventors they regard as having potential to turn a profit, ideally a big profit. In the game, we use a virtual (make-believe) currency called "Monkey." The investors invest by buying the stocks of inventors they favor. The winner of the game is the investor who has the stock with the highest value at the end. It is important for the investors to evaluate the talent of each inventor by listening carefully to new ideas because they are ultimately judged by the value of the stock they hold. The higher an inventor is rated by the investors, the more expensive his/her stock will be because the price of each stock is set by the law of supply and demand: a balance between the investors' willingness to buy and the inventor's willingness to sell. If an investor has invested in an inventor and wants to make him or her more popular, the investor needs to give the inventor hints for creating useful/sellable ideas, and must also sometimes provide constructive criticism to improve certain ideas. The improved communication between players by involving investors ultimately resulted in improved ideas.

6.5   Consumers: The Evaluators of Idea Quality

When we added investors to IMG and continued with the trial games, we found ourselves with a new gaming style in which new ideas were obtained and improved via the communication between players who represent the two kinds of stakeholders required for innovation. Although we were able to obtain new ideas that satisfied both parties, a disconcerting problem remained: Would such ideas also satisfy the members of a real marketplace? At the time, we could not say yes: the inventors did not always consider the actual utility of the ideas presented by the inventors. We noticed that although the goal of the inventors should be to satisfy both the existing and latent requirements of consumers, this was not reinforced by the investors. In spite of players' requests for simplicity, we decided to add consumers as a third party of core players in order to obtain novel ideas that are actually required by real society.

The role of consumers is to choose interesting ideas from the pool of proposed ideas and buy them after negotiating a price. The consumers are awarded their final scores after being evaluated on how their lives change after buying the ideas. This evaluation is performed by examining their lifestyles, both during and after the game. If their lifestyles improve enough they can win the game, so consumers should also give the inventors hints for new ideas and constructive criticism for improving the proposed ideas. In this process, each consumer should be even more earnest than investors because they have to explain why and how the purchase of ideas improved their quality of life.

We often introduce *sub-roles* of consumers, such as "students," "the elderly," "homemaker" etc., one of which each consumer should choose as early as possible in the game. This is to make them conscious of real contexts in life so that they can evaluate ideas from a more realistic and concrete point of view. Note there is another participant in IMG, who is the dealer of the game. However, he/she appears mainly just as the distributor of items (cards, money, etc.) for gaming, as reader will find in the following. Although doing a dealer may have an effect to train the talent of organizing a communication space, we are not going deep into this effect.

6.6   A Model of Communications Between Stakeholders

What is the essential difference between investors and consumers? To start with, the investors evaluate the ability of each inventor to think up new ideas, and those who have been highly trained in the real business world tend to pay attention to the quality, not just the quantity, of ideas. Such "good" investors listen to the inventors' presentations and evaluate the feasibility of applying their vision to the real market. However, a good investor does not always win the game, because the stock prices fluctuate on the basis of the other investors' behaviors. In addition, most of the investors seem to assume that inventors with a greater number of ideas may try harder to get the investors' attention. That is, if most investors in the game are inclined to invest in an inventor who presents ideas frequently, easily affected by their enthusiasm, the stock price of such an inventor will grow rapidly. If so, it is not a good idea for an investor to listen carefully to each idea presented by an inventor who speaks slowly or infrequently. As a result, the inventors' stock prices inevitably rise in relation to the number of their idea proposals. Thus, it is

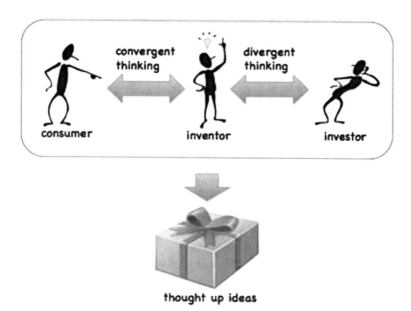

Fig. 6.1 A model of stakeholders' communication in the Innovators' Market Game

beneficial for investors to stimulate divergent thought and communications in the game: the frequent appearance of ideas is the fuel of communication even if the ideas themselves are trivial, and this makes it worthwhile to continue the communication.

In contrast, the consumers by necessity evaluate the quality of each idea. The consumers do not care about the number of ideas proposed by each inventor in the slightest: after all, a good idea from a calm person like Henry Ford is much better than a joke from a comedian or a wild, impossible scenario from an eloquent speaker. Thus, the consumers listen carefully to each presentation in their hunt for the best ideas. To put it simply, we can say that consumers encourage convergent (as opposed to the investors' divergent) thought and communications to find ideas that can be used by actual people.

In order to convince the consumers to buy their ideas, the inventors must have a vision, that is, a context in which they create ideas. They need to specify their business areas, which correspond to the domains of knowledge they use, or their market domains. Thus, by adding consumers to IMG, new, relevant ideas are obtained through communications between the three types of stakeholders (provided the players understand their missions): inventors who have explicit or tacit knowledge of basic technologies and concepts in the market, investors who prefer high-frequency proposals, and consumers who place importance on inventors' vision and talk honestly about their desires.

Figure 6.1 shows a simplified model of the communication between the three types of players. Previous studies on creativity support have also shown that both divergence and convergence are necessary to obtain novel and useful ideas (see for example (Plattner et al. 2010)): divergence is required for novelty and convergence for utility. Both thinking stages must be interwoven with each other. In IMG, the communication between inventors and investors ideally encourages divergent thinking for new ideas while that between inventors and consumers encourages convergent thinking. By including these three roles in the game, IMG evolved into an established system for generating innovation through communication between stakeholders.

6.7   The Basic Items Used in IMG

In this section, we describe how to actually play IMG. Figure 6.2 shows a group of business people playing IMG to seek out new visions and ideas for collaborative business. (We shall return to this photograph in Chap. 8 when we discuss some actual cases.) As seen in the figure, there are various items that need to be prepared for the game:

- A set of *basic cards* showing pieces of basic knowledge
- Notes of the virtual "Monkey" currency
- Large sticky labels
- Small sticky labels
- Small slips of paper for use as stocks

Fig. 6.2 Playing IMG

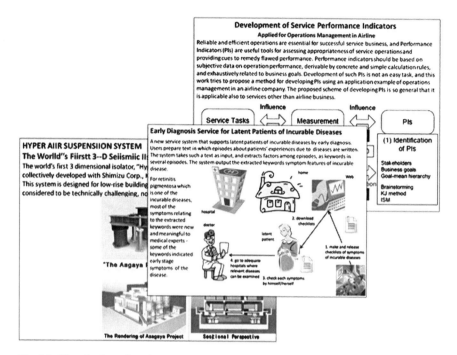

Fig. 6.3 Three basic cards to be combined for thinking up ideas

- A game board
- Bunches of sub-role cards

The first item is a set of basic cards describing the summary of existing knowledge about technologies, products, services, and business models that will eventually be combined in various ways by inventors to propose new ideas. About 30–50 basic cards are produced. Figure 6.3 shows an example of basic cards on up-to-date technologies relevant to computers, space engineering, and city engineering. Each basic card shows the title of the existing knowledge as well as a brief description of it and a photograph. Having the limited number of basic cards in advance succeeds the discovery of Finke we mentioned in the previous chapter – the pre-inventive knowledge (structures) should be limited.

The inventors buy however many of these cards they need to propose their new ideas. Each card costs one Monkey (see Fig. 6.4) if selected randomly from the prepared pool of cards and two Monkeys if the inventor requests it by title. Inventors can buy basic cards at any time during the game. Investors and consumers also use Monkey notes to buy stocks or ideas at any time during the game.

If an inventor comes up with a new idea, he/she writes the idea on a large sticky label. Each inventor has his/her own color of label to distinguish between them, e.g., "inventor Red," "inventor Blue," etc. An example of these labels, each with one idea, is shown in Fig. 6.5. This figure also shows another kind of small cards, called

Fig. 6.4 Virtual (toy) currency called "Monkey." Used to buy basic cards and to invest in and buy proposed ideas

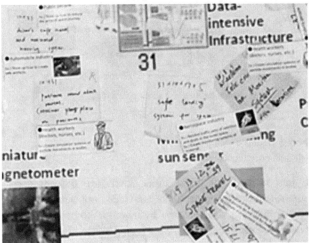

Fig. 6.5 Large labels for writing ideas. The ID numbers of the basic cards used for a new idea are also written (e.g., "safe landing system for space" in the center was created by combining ideas 31, 10, 7, and 5). This picture was taken after the completion of a game and shows all of the basic cards that had been put on the board during the game

sub-role cards, placed by consumers on ideas they have bought. When choosing their sub-role, as mentioned in Sect. 6.5, consumers should take one bunch (10 or 15) of sub-role cards, from which they eventually select one when buying. Inventors also stick small labels on the basic cards they possess to express their ownership. Figure 6.6 shows an example of small labels stuck on the basic cards that each inventor has bought. Small slips are used as toy stock corresponding to the inventors. At the beginning of each game, the dealer gives each inventor a predetermined number of the slips, which they then sell to investors.

Fig. 6.6 A scene from IMG. Labels are used to distinguish the owners of basic cards and the inventors of created ideas

Earnest players – particularly inventors – tend to want to know which basic cards are available and which are suitable for combining with the basic cards they currently possess. In order to satisfy these desires, they can use a game board on which a graph is drawn visualizing the relationships among pieces of basic knowledge. The basic cards are shown in the graph as nodes and the relationships as edges. We use a data crystallization algorithm (Horie et al. 2007; Ohsawa 2005) to evaluate the relationships. An example of the game board is shown in Fig. 6.7. The inventors put their basic cards on the board to help them think up new ideas by getting hints about which basic cards are easy to combine or which might create novel ideas. Roughly speaking, basic cards that are relevant to each other are easy to combine because they share the same context (such as "commodities for washing tableware" or "items for healthcare"), but on the other hand, cards with weak relevance, which are difficult to combine, may create a novel, interesting idea. For example, a cup and a plate are easy to combine to create "a dinner set," which is neither novel nor interesting. However, if the inventor adds a hammer (normally irrelevant to a dinner set), the tableware can turn into a musical instrument in which various cups and plates make interesting sounds. If the inventor has the basic cards of a cup and a plate and finds a hammer at a node in the graph being indirectly linked to a cup and plate, he can buy the basic hammer card. Throughout the entire game, the small labels are useful for showing who owns which basic cards, giving each player a bird's-eye view of the other player's interests.

6.8 How to Play the Game

It takes about 3 h for playing IMG, including 2 h of actual gaming. For the first 30 min, the dealer assigns each player a role and explains the rules of the game. It is best according to our experiences if there are three or four players for each part

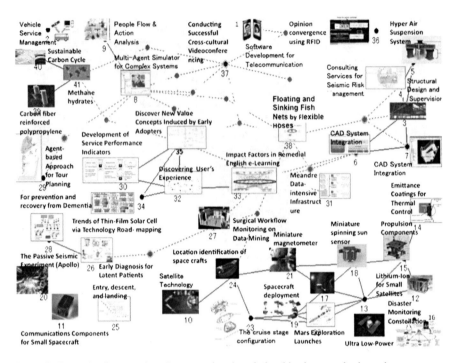

Fig. 6.7 Example of a game board representing the relationships between basic cards

(inventor, investor, and consumer). We recommend about 10 players per game so that all players have an equal opportunity to give their opinions, thus improving the chances of generating ideas satisfactory to all players. After explaining the rules, the dealer gives an equal amount of money (about 10 Monkeys) to each player. Then the game starts.

At first, the inventors should buy their initial basic cards, which they can also buy at any time during the game. They can buy as many cards as they like so long as they have sufficient funds. After a card is bought, an inventor attaches a small label to it and then puts the basic card on the corresponding node on the graph (the game board) to facilitate thinking up of ideas by combining existing techniques written on their cards. When inventors think up a new idea, they write it on a large label of the color corresponding to their identity (e.g., inventor Red writes on a red label). Inventors can use others' cards if they successfully negotiate for them, for example, by borrowing them or swapping with one of their own cards.

After an inventor writes down an idea and puts the large label on the board, he/she verbally proposes the idea to the other players (see Figs. 6.5 and 6.6). The investors and the consumers listen to the proposal and when it is finished they evaluate and critique it. All players can join this discussion, the aim of which is to identify hidden merits or defects so that the idea can be improved. At any time – during the discussion or after it is finished – the investors can invest money in the inventor and the consumers can buy the idea. Inventors can propose new ideas or buy new cards at any time, as well. In an average game, which should last about 2 h, we expect inventors to propose around 15–30 ideas.

Finally, the game ends and the winners are announced. The inventors are evaluated by their income (the number of Monkey notes they possess), the investors are evaluated by the total worth of their stock (the sum of the number of slips they possess and their prices), and the consumers are evaluated based on their presentations on how their lifestyles have been improved by applying the bought ideas to their lives. In cases when sub-role cards are used, the presentation should be from the viewpoint of the role the consumer selected. There are three winners: the inventor and investor with the highest incomes, and the consumer who obtains the most approval from other players. The process of determining and announcing the winners takes about 30 min, and after that, the game is wrapped up.

6.9   The Game Board Supporting Players

As in Fig. 6.7, the game board used in IMG visualizes the relationships between the basic cards as a graph by the data crystallization, which was discussed in Chap. 3. The map obtained by data crystallization gives the players hints by means of various embedded information.

We first added the game board to IMG at the beginning of 2009. There were three central reasons for this addition. First, it is necessary for the players to know which basic cards are available, and what the relationships between the cards are, as we have already mentioned. The second reason is that visualization is useful in terms of understanding what kinds of ideas are proposed on the basis of which basic cards, and how the new ideas are distributed and connected with each other in the market of ideas. That is, the players can grasp the positioning of each idea and if it is a basic card or a fully formed idea indicated by a large colored label.

The third and most important reason is that the bridge (red in the original software, or gray in this book) nodes give players hints for thinking up new ideas. The information given by these bridge nodes is considered useful for thinking up innovative ideas, as in the application case of data crystallization we showed in Chap. 3. That is, if an inventor combines basic cards that are connected via red (gray in this book) nodes, there is a high likelihood that they will come up with a valuable idea.

There are also reasons which may seem peripheral but are really important: If players did not use the game board, they would tend to concentrate on obtaining high incomes rather than on proposing new and innovative ideas because they would not have effective guidelines for obtaining new ideas. By applying the game board, players can focus on thinking about existing and new ideas because the basic cards reflect each moment in the process of idea creation, and each moment is reflected by the labels stuck on the game board and the memory of players about all the actions. Players can see which cards have been used and by whom, and because they share the same target to see and manipulate, they can cultivate their ideas together.

6.10   A Trial Case of IMG: Household Commodities

We have tested our game more than 100 times in businesses, universities, school festivals, and in political settings. The users have included students, faculty members, experts in atomic technology, and more. In this section, we show some brief examples of trial games to give the reader an idea of the flow of the game. More practical cases will be presented in greater depth in Chaps. 8 and 9. Table 6.1 shows a list of the basic cards for household commodities, Fig. 6.8 shows a game board made from the basic cards by applying the data crystallization algorithm. See Fig. 6.9, showing a scene of IMG. As a result of IMG, the game board gets pasted with stick labels and cards as in Fig. 6.10. Table 6.2 shows examples of the obtained ideas.

6.11   The Open Problem Addressed in the Following Chapters

In summary, find the IMG rule table in Table 6.3. Most of the players seemed to have a good time during the game (see Fig. 6.9), and several highly evaluated ideas were obtained. However, when we interviewed players about the quality of each idea again after the game, we often found that ideas that had previously been highly evaluated were now regarded as low-novelty or low-utility and thus not adaptable to real business. For example, during the game, the idea about a portable shower for

Table 6.1 Some of the basic cards made for household commodities

The name of basic card	Description
(1) Paper carton clip	When a paper carton of milk is opened, you can use it to clip the carton firmly shut. The milk will not spill out, even if the carton is on its side. The clipped carton can easily be stored in a fridge, keeping the milk fresh
(2) Cupuled soap holder	There are a lot of suckers in the holder so that it can be firmly fixed to slippery things. It's also easy to peel off
(3) Power mat	It's made of synthetic rubber, and its heat-proof temperature is 150°C! It has wide applications. For example, it can be used as a pot holder, or you can use it to wrest open a jar or bottle that is difficult to turn. It can also be used to hold the hot handle of a pan
(Skip 4–10)	
(11) Eye training glasses	There are a lot of small holes in the glasses. When you look through the holes, your eyes can be trained to prevent or calibrate near-sightedness and far-sightedness. It's easier to use than you think!
(Skip 12–29)	
(30) Ironing glove	This is a good helper when ironing. Clothes can be directly ironed while draped on a hanger. Try it once!

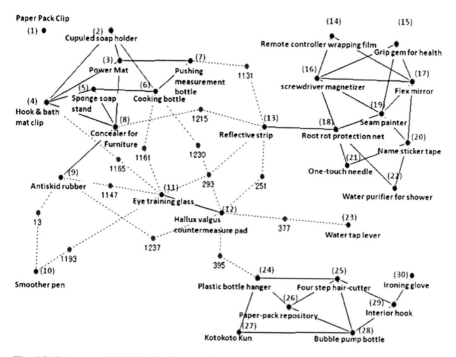

Fig. 6.8 Data-crystallized KeyGraph made from information of household consumption of products in Japanese 100 yen (about 1 dollar) shops. The nodes with numbers (1131, 251, etc.) are dummies. The original board was in Japanese

Fig. 6.9 The effect of visualization: Players see and touch the same things

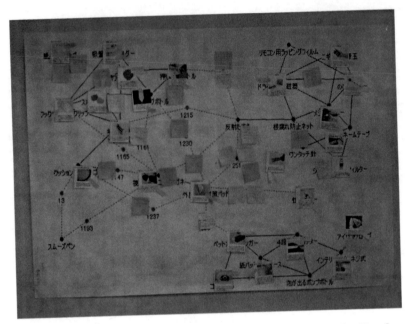

Fig. 6.10 The game board as a result of IMG. The game board in Fig. 6.8 translated into Japanese is used here

Table 6.2 Proposed ideas combining household commodities that were highly evaluated

Proposed idea	Card 1	Card 2
T-shirt shaped ironing board	Interior hook	Ironing glove
Granularity-flexible scissors. You can change the granularity of the scissor teeth depending on the desired level	Shredder scissors	four-step hair-cutter
Cupuled kettle. You do not need to be afraid of knocking over a kettle	Cupuled soap holder	Microwave oven simple kettle
Funny glasses. You can make people laugh by squeezing mayonnaise from the holes in the glasses	Eye training glasses	Cooking bottle
A device for cleaning narrow spaces	Flex mirror	Glass flashing (wiper)
Hook for drying out paper cartons	Hook and bath mat clip	Paper carton clip
Portable shower for outside	Plastic bottle hanger	Water purifier for shower

Table 6.3 The rules of IMG

Dealer	Inventors	Consumers	Investors
1. Hold the basic cards	Receive 10 M (Monkey)	Receive 10 M	Receive 10 M
2. Distribute money to players			
	Start the game: The following can be done at any time during the game		
4. Game management: Encourage speaking, such as criticism and declarations of intentions and constraints	Purchase basic cards from dealer: 1 M for random choice. 2 M for a specific card and/or from others by negotiating the price	Choose a role card, after observing the progress of the game. Then, continue: Buy a desired product/service, if the price negotiation with its inventor is successful. *Put your role card on the idea (label) you bought	Stock-trade following dealer's advice: Negotiate with inventors or with other investors to buy a suitable amount of stocks
Connect a new idea P with basic cards A, B, C, …, used to propose P by drawing lines, if inventors do not	Write a new idea P, on a label of your personal color, from the combination of basic cards. Also write the IDs of combined basic cards. Basic cards and the labels should be put on the corresponding positions on the game board	Ask, talk, and interact with inventors! You are likely to win if you buy ideas that come close to your goals. Therefore, make free comments on investors' ideas: either criticism or evaluation. Consumers and investors may certainly suggest new ideas to inventors, and demand a reward for the suggestions	
	Stop the game (1 or 2 h from the start)		
5. Scoring and wrapping up	Score = the earned money. *The basic cards in hand are regarded as 0 M. If this seems unfair, use up your cards!	Presentation: Explain goals (requirements) you set yourself, and how much of the goal has been achieved by the ideas you bought. The score is determined by evaluations from other players, or the number of players who raise hands to "Do you think a valuable goal has been achieved?"	Score = money + total worth of stocks

outdoor use was evaluated as highly demanded, highly feasible, and highly novel. However, we were not able to obtain information about the outside environment, and we did not know whether or not it was possible to have a portable shower outside. Even if it is possible, we need to identify suitable outdoor places for hanging the shower bag. We do not need a hanger if there are trees, and we cannot use the shower if it is in the city. Basically, we could not always discuss potential user demands in detail.

In order to translate an idea into actual society, we must resolve several constraints existing around the idea. It is difficult to identify the constraints during and just after the game because players are usually excited and caught up in the play. Although this problem remained an open problem for a while, we came up with some solutions, which we will present shortly. We have presented IMG at academic conferences (Ohsawa 2008; Ohsawa and Nishihara 2010; Wang and Ohsawa 2011), but we introduced IMG more seriously and successfully in real workplaces as a result of and as a reason for obtaining the solutions presented in the following sections.

References

Horie K, Maeno Y, Ohsawa Y (2007) Data crystallization applied to desinging new products. J Syst Sci Syst Eng 16(1):34–49

Ohsawa Y (2005) Data crystallization: chance discovery extended for dealing with unobservable events. New Math Nat Comput 1(3):373–392

Ohsawa Y (2008) Chance discovery and chance creation: a data-visualization approach to value sensitive innovation. In: Proceedings of the Second Asia international conference on modeling and simulation, Kuala Lumpur

Ohsawa Y, Nishihara Y (2010) Innovators marketplace: process of games as a service system of, by, and for innovators. Proceedings on the international workshop on innovating service systems(ISS2010), pp 115–124, Tokyo

Plattner H, Meinel C, Leifer L (2010) Design thinking: understand-improve-apply. Springer, Heidelberg

Wang H, Ohsawa Y (2011). Ideas discovery as extension of chance discovery for advanced market innovation. The 2011 SIAM international workshop on data mining for marketing, Mesa

Chapter 7
Evidence-Based Guidelines for Innovators' Marketplace

7.1 Game Board Showing Niches in the Idea Market

7.1.1 Experimental Method

We have tested out the Innovators' Market Game using several different types of players. For example, in some games, all the players were from our School of Engineering (The University of Tokyo), while in others, the players consisted of students from across multiple disciplines (engineering, economics, law, etc.), or business people from multiple sections of a company (research, product design/development, marketing, etc.). We also tried open games where students and business people joined anonymously.

In all games, our most important finding was that IMG provides an enjoyable environment for innovative thought – in stark contrast to the workplace, where individuals are forced to think of new ideas for the sake of their section. This is significant in terms of application to real business, because being forced to think impedes free conversation where tacit knowledge acquired from daily experiences can be externalized, and it also limits the production of ideas for future scenarios. Even worse, many individuals get the feeling that their ideas may have an negative effect on their income or chances for promotion because they tend to reject others' criticisms even if the comments might have been helpful in improving the idea. All of this highlights the importance of giving workers a motivation that does not involve coercion or other negative pressure.

In the experimental games described thus far, we collected the following data on the behaviors of players:

(**Data set 1**) Videotaped scenes of all games. These showed the voices and actions of the players and the dealer and included the presentation of ideas and the buying/selling of ideas and stocks.

Y. Ohsawa and Y. Nishihara, *Innovators' Marketplace*, Understanding Innovation,
DOI 10.1007/978-3-642-25480-2_7, © Springer-Verlag Berlin Heidelberg 2012

(Data set 2)   The score of each idea. Both investors and consumers evaluated the
quality of each created idea after the game on the basis of "novelty," "utility
(consumer demand)," "earning power," "reality," etc.

(Data set 3)   A hand-written description of the created ideas. During each game,
ideas were marked A, B, C, etc., with the letters corresponding to the order of
the presentations.

(Data set 4)   The ideas or knowledge (in the basic cards) combined to create each
idea in **Data set 3**.

By looking at these datasets as a whole, we can investigate the effect of various
elements of a particular game on the quality of the obtained ideas. For example,
we were able to determine the effect of the visualized game board and of criticisms
and empathetic utterances (rather than negotiation utterances) on idea quality, as we
shall see later in this chapter.

Initially, the most basic trend we observed in this project was that the quality
of ideas tended to increase with time. The quality was defined by *novelty* ×
reality where the novelty and reality (how realistic the idea is, considering various
conditions such as cost, time, the current state of technologies and social situations,
etc.) tended to change in a trade-off relationship – i.e., one increases when the
other decreases – but both are necessary for realizing innovation in a global
environment in which a concrete contribution to sustainable social welfare is
demanded. However, this quality-increase trend was not always evident. Thus, we
focused on the temporal effect: that is, previously presented ideas affecting ideas
created afterward. What we mean here is that the increase of scores may be an
effect of previously presented ideas, and that the fizzling out of idea creation that
comes at the end of a game might be the effect of saturation caused by the rash of
ideas. Actually, the decrease trend is typically found in cases where highly scored
ideas were sustained throughout the entire time.

At this point, we turned to several hypotheses reflecting creativity theories in
past studies and our own experiences in chance discovery. For example, we know
that innovation comes from the combination of existing ideas, as we discussed
in Chap. 4. Some other theories insist that ambiguous information and suitable
questions are what spur creativity in design. If we interpret these concepts roughly
and connect them to the visualized game board, in a manner similar to the one
we discussed in Chap. 3, we may be able to expect that a combination of items in
black clusters (corresponding to frequent items and concepts) via red nodes results
in innovation because existing knowledge is combined via items with ambiguity.
That is, it is ambiguous and uncertain to judge to which black cluster and the red
nodes are relevant, because they can be regarded as the niche between established
trends.

In this section, we discuss the relation of niche ideas to innovation. For example,
Figs. 7.1 and 7.2 shows the two different types of niches. In Fig. 7.1, a created idea
is put on a free space, i.e., not at any node in or between clusters, from which items
were chosen and combined for creation. The clusters do include other ideas which
have been previously used (see the small labels attached close to the nodes, where

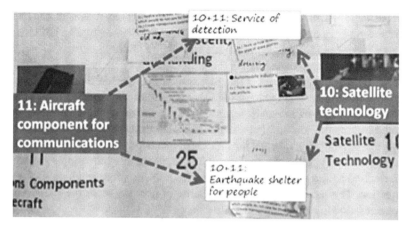

Fig. 7.1 Free niche ideas: without connections via links on the graph

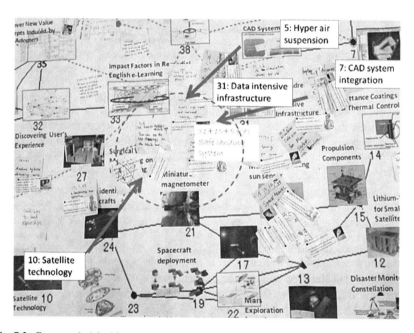

Fig. 7.2 Connected niche ideas: connected via dotted lines to black nodes (The same as Fig. 7.1)

basic cards were placed during play). Figure 7.2 shows the other type of niche, where a new idea has been presented at a red node in the graph, which is between clusters, including basic cards that have already been used.

Let us call the former type – an idea created by combining ideas in clusters not connected via links but including already-used basic cards – a "free niche" idea, and the latter type – an idea created at a node connecting nodes in cluster(s), including already-used basic cards, via links in the graph – a "connected niche" idea. We can tell what type of idea has been created by combining ideas in those clusters using the hand-written data showing a list of ideas a particular player used for the creation (Data set 3 above). A niche can be regarded as a combination of ideas for innovation, as stated in previous studies, but a niche here also means that the combined ideas had been used when thinking and the process of incubating ideas had already started. As illustrated by the examples in Chap. 3, the prepared mind favoring a chance can be interpreted as the experiences and thoughts pooled before catching a new clue for creation. The theorization of making sense of new events as the framework of analogical reasoning can be reviewed in Chap. 4.

In the procedure described below, we evaluated ideas and placed them into one of six types of niche. First, in preparation, we had the quality of each idea evaluated in terms of its novelty and reality. Then, all ideas were removed from the game board (the KeyGraph graph) and then placed back on the board one by one. We performed steps (1)–(3) (below) each time an idea was created.

(1) Categorization of each idea presented: Each time an idea T was created on the game board, conditions X and Y were checked as follows.

  - X: The extent to which the ideas combined for creating T belonged to clusters including ideas in set U, the set of ideas used by the time (2: Yes, all the combined ideas belonged, 0: No, none of the combined ideas did, 1: between 0 and 2, i.e., some but not all of the ideas combined for creating T belonged to such clusters).
  - Y: Whether the idea was put on an existing red/black node/line. Idea T is categorized by X and Y: If X is 2, 1, or 0, then T is *between activated clusters (i.e., in a niche), partially between activated clusters, or between newly activated clusters*, respectively. If Y is no, T is free. If Y is yes, then T is connected.

(2) Attach missing links: When there is no suitable node on the game board on which to put the created idea, the player can put it on a free space - i.e., one without nodes - but we should manually draw a new red line connecting the created idea to the clusters including the combined basic ideas.

(3) Cluster revision: If there are multiple clusters that have been connected via red lines (drawn automatically or manually), and which have so far contributed to creating the same ideas by combining belonging ideas, the clusters are unified into one cluster.

After this procedure, all presented ideas in five experimental games were classified into six classes corresponding to the three values of X and the two values of Y. Then, for all the ideas in each class, the evaluated scores were checked and the five ideas with the highest scores for each game were counted (see Table 7.1). We found that the "between activated clusters" (ideas in the niches) tended to

Table 7.1 The five highest-scored ideas in two types of niche: average (standard deviation)

	Between activated clusters (niche)	Partially between activated clusters	Between newly activated clusters
Free	0.40 (0.42)	0.04 (0.09)	0.1 (0.22)
Connected	0.26 (0.15)	0.17 (0.24)	0 (0)

include ideas with the highest scores, although the standard deviation was high. There were also differences between the free and connected niches for the five highest-score ideas, but this tendency is the opposite between the first and second columns.

Tendency 1:   The ideas "between activated clusters" i.e., ideas in the niches, tended to have the highest scores.

Tendency 2:   The free niches tended to include especially highly scored ideas, but the deviation was high: the reliability of the ideas presented in free spaces was low.

Tendency 3:   The connected niches tended to include relatively highly scored ideas, and the deviation was low: the reliability of the ideas presented at nodes connected to clusters including previously used ideas was high.

From these tendencies, we can recommend that players be patient until ideas have been created from combinations of ideas in clusters (as in the right side of Fig. 7.3), without expecting high scores, in the early stages of the game. Players will eventually be enabled to create good ideas if they focus on the niches of activated ideas. If a particular player wants a high score and does not mind taking risks for the chance of a hit, the free space between clusters including activated ideas is recommended. In contrast, if a player is more cautious and likes certainty (hedging the risk of low score), positioning ideas on nodes or lines on the graph is better.

In real tests of this game in companies, where the players aim to develop real innovation for real products or services, it is not easy to maintain patience while waiting for clusters to become occupied by activated ideas. Also, in some cases, they prefer to combine new ideas (in clusters missing used/activated ideas) with used ideas. In such a case, the player should take especial note of the tendency below, which is based on the middle column of Table 7.1:

Tendency 4:   The node that combines ideas, some of which are from (i.e., partially between) activated clusters and others from non-activated clusters, where the clusters are connected via red nodes, promises better ideas than a free space between partially activated clusters. That is, if one prefers to combine ideas from clusters both with and without activated ideas, we recommend creating an idea on a node connecting these clusters (Ohsawa and Nishihara 2009).

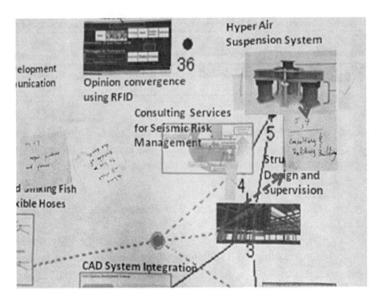

Fig. 7.3 The easiest way to think: work in one popular island

7.2 Recommendable Consciousness in Communication (I): Empathy for Enhancing Novelty

So far, we have facilitated more than 100 IMG games, and players have told us that they feel their communications skills and ability to create socially useful knowledge for business was elevated both during and after the game. After the games and the consumer presentation evaluations are completed, the quality of the created ideas is evaluated by all investors and reviewers on criteria such as "novelty", "cost", "utility", and "reality". We found a significant relation between the players' communication and the evaluated quality of ideas. Our data on the player utterances showed that the novelty and utility of ideas are strongly related to each other and tend to significantly increase (1) after an increase in empathetic utterances by investors/consumers and (2) before the appearance of a sequence of negative utterances, i.e., criticisms, followed by a positive utterance. Here, an empathetic utterance means a comment concretely referring to the proposed use scene of the presented idea. These results suggest that innovative communication comes from (1) the context sharing induced by the visualized graph, and (2) the interest of all participants in revising the presented ideas. We will present some data to illustrate these tendencies in this and the next sections.

As mentioned in Chap. 2, cognitive empathy is not a disembodied and affectless "knowing of the other" but rather the feeling of being led by another's experiences. Here, "feeling" means the integrated sense of bodily sensation and emotional values. We therefore take "empathetic utterance" to mean a comment that concretely expressing the value conclusion (either positive or negative) of an idea with respect

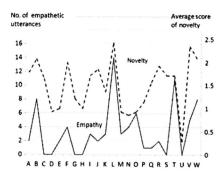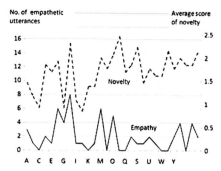

Fig. 7.4 The correlation of changes in empathetic utterances and novelty scores (two games). The horizontal axis shows the ideas sorted by time from the *left* to the *right*

to the use scene proposed by someone else. For example, "Any doctor who uses the bottle you propose might lose it because it is very small" is regarded as just as empathetic "If I were a doctor, I would use your bottle." On the other hand, "What's the point of this bottle for me? I'm a student, not a doctor" is not empathetic because the use scene proposed by the inventor (in a hospital by a doctor) is ignored. "Let's hear the next idea" and "I'll buy your idea for ten Monkeys" are not at all empathetic.

Figure 7.4 shows the changes in the number of empathetic utterances exchanged after each new idea was proposed from the beginning to the end of two games. As you can see, the originality of ideas tends to increase shortly after empathetic utterances. We investigated all the utterances in five games, and four games showed the correspondence (co-occurrence within two sequentially presented ideas) between the fastest increase in the number of empathetic utterances and in the score of novelty, where the novelty of each idea (A, B, C, ...) was scored between 0 and 3 by all investors after the game. The average score given by all referees is shown in Fig. 7.4.

These results may seem at odds with the intuition of the reader: proposing a new use scene, which is quite different from the inventors' proposal, might be expected to prompt the inventor to view the same idea from a different viewpoint, thereby encouraging creativity. However, in reality, a comment that jumps to a new context tends to either be ignored or to interrupt thoughtful communication if thrown in before players have thought and communicated enough following the proposed use scene. Thus, we recommend that players not jump to a new use scene before others are satisfied with thinking and talking about the current scene.

7.3 Recommendable Consciousness in Communication (II): Criticism for Enhancing Utility

In the game, inventors not only propose ideas but also improve on ideas by reflecting on comments from the investors, thus illustrating how communication helps improve ideas. Comments are made for all ideas, although some of the ideas are evaluated highly and receive large investments while others do not. Here, we show our analysis of communications between the players in order to find exactly which type of utterances improve ideas to the point that they are highly evaluated (Nishihara and Ohsawa 2010). In particular, we focus on negative comments, i.e., criticisms.

We analyzed the communications manually. First, we transcribed the communications from the recorded videotape into text and divided the text into several sections, each including the proposal of an idea (the presentation by an inventor). We manually annotated utterances with tags in order to identify their type and then visualized the tag transitions. Finally, we isolated the communication features that signaled an idea would be highly valued.

We set four tags for utterances reflecting a speaking player's attitude: positive (P), neutral (I), negative (N), and just laughing (L). The P tag was attached to an utterance showing a positive reaction to the previous utterance, for example, when a player answered "Yes" to a question. The I tag was attached to an utterance without even an air of evaluating the previous utterance, for example, when a player answered a question about what the idea was used for, or which cards were used. We attached the L tag to utterances that were made up of laughter (note: laughter is not always humorous in Japan, but sometimes implies weak evaluation which may be negative). The N tag was attached to an utterance exhibiting a negative reaction to the previous utterance. We further classified N tags into four sub-types:

- N1: An emotional interjection from an investor who does not understand or does not accept a presented idea
- N2: A sentence mentioning the extent to which an investor does not understand or accept a presented idea
- N3: A question implying a negative evaluation of a previous utterance
- N4: An indication that an idea has obvious deficiencies

Table 7.2 shows some examples of utterances corresponding to these negative tags. Since N1 or N2 do not represent a total dismissal of an idea's utility, the possibility of improving the idea is expected. However, utterances annotated with N1 tags do not include any suggestions for improving ideas, and as an obvious result these ideas are seldom improved. N3 and the N4 tags, in contrast, represent the strong disapproval of an idea. The purpose of this analysis is to determine how N2 utterances relate to improved ideas, and to compare these with N3 and N4 utterances. Specifically, we analyzed the relationships between these negative tags and the amount of investment given to ideas. We defined "highly-invested" as an idea to which the amount of invested money was larger than the average plus the standard deviation of investments to ideas in one game.

For five games (the relevant data of which is summarized in Tables 7.3 and 7.4), where the players and basic cards varied from game to game, we analyzed items as follows: (1) the relationship between the investment to and the number of utterances in an idea proposal, (2) the relationship between investment and utterance tags, and (3) the relationship between the investment and the transitions from/to tags in the discourse.

Table 7.2 Examples of negative utterance for each tag

Tag	Player	Utterance
N1	Inventor	We expect to use it in education
	Investor	Hmm ...
N2	Inventor	I propose an idea
	Investor	I can't understand your idea because it seems implausible
N3	Inventor	We can use all of the energy until the Earth dies
	Investor	What do you use for huge quantities of energy?
N4	Inventor	Here is my proposal, although I must admit the idea has some problems
	Investor	Your idea about small computers does not consider data security. I would be wary of using such a computer

Table 7.3 Analyzed IMG data

Game	No. of inventors	No. of investors	No. of obtained ideas	No. of ideas that received a high investment
1	3	3	16	1
2	4	3	20	3
3	4	8	13	2
4	4	8	13	2
5	3	6	17	3

Table 7.4 Averages and standard deviations of the investment amounts

Game	Average	Standard deviation	Average + standard deviation
1	1.2	2.6	3.7
2	4.3	4.1	8.4
3	3.5	2.3	5.8
4	5.1	4.4	9.5
5	8.6	7.9	16.6

Table 7.5 Averages and variances of utterances in communications

	High investment	Low investment
Average no. of utterances	42.8	23.5
Variance of no. of utterances	12.9	16.9

The relationship between the investment to and the number of utterances in an idea proposal (Table 7.5)

The average number of utterances for highly invested ideas was larger than the average for other ideas ($t = 4.2$, $p = 0.00087 < 0.1$). The average number of utterances from innovators was 22.2 and the average from investors was 20.8; there is no significant difference ($t = 1.3$, $p = 0.19 > 0.1$). These results indicate that if players communicate for a long time, the generated ideas tend to receive high investments.

The relationship between investment and utterance tags (Fig. 7.5)

The rate of positive utterances for highly invested ideas was higher than the rate for other ideas (Chi-squared $= 85.4$, $p = 2.2e - 16 < 0.1$, $r = 9.00$). The rate of

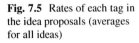

Fig. 7.5 Rates of each tag in the idea proposals (averages for all ideas)

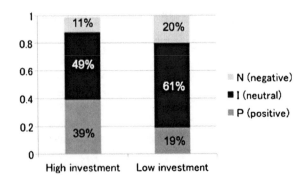

positive utterances from innovators was 0.4 while from investors it was 0.38; again, no significant difference. These results indicate that positive utterances encourage the generation of highly invested ideas.

The rate of negative utterances for ideas that were not highly invested was higher than the rate for those that were (Chi-squared $= 85.4$, $p = 2.2e - 16 < 0.1$, $r = 4.37$). Although the rate of negative utterances from innovators was 0.16, the rate of negative utterances from investors was 0.31, which represents a significant difference ($t = 5.05$, $p = 0.000014 < 0.1$). These results indicate that many negative utterances from investors translate into a lower chance of investment.

The relationship between investment and tag transitions

Figure 7.6 shows an example of a tag transition in a communication in which an idea was invested with a lot of money, while Fig. 7.7 shows a contrasting example of a tag transition in a communication in which an idea received no investment. The vertical axis denotes an utterance tag and the horizontal axis denotes which player made the utterance. In the case shown in Fig. 7.6, there were many positive utterances, including the final utterance. In contrast, in the case shown in Fig. 7.7, the communication alternated between positive and negative utterances, and the final utterance was a negative one.

The curves in these figures show that the transitions for ideas that received either high or low investments were different. We defined 11 patterns of transition (shown in Table 7.6) and counted the number of ideas with transitions in each pattern. Here, we detected two kinds of transition: divergence and convergence. The convergence is a sequence in which the same tag appears more than four times in a row, and the divergence is a sequence in which this does not occur. Divergence is further classified into two types: a sequence starting from a negative/neutral tag followed by a positive tag, and a sequence starting from a neutral/positive tag followed by a negative tag (see Fig. 7.8). The results we obtained are shown in Table 7.6.

An example of a transition for an idea that received a high investment ((6) in Table 7.6) is shown in Table 7.7. Investors made negative utterances about the risk of ozone in utterance Nos. 2 and 4. An inventor then responded with an utterance about the ozone risk in No. 5. Rounds between positive and negative utterances appeared in this communication. Since the investors ultimately accepted

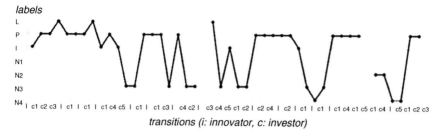

transitions (i: innovator, c: investor)

Fig. 7.6 An example of tag transition for an idea that received a high investment

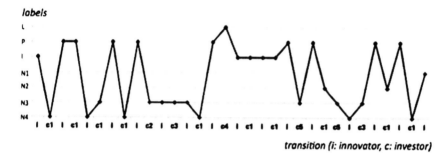

transition (i: innovator, c: investor)

Fig. 7.7 An example of tag transition for an idea that received a low investment

Table 7.6 Tag transition and the number of ideas that had high or low investment rates. C and D denote convergence and divergence, respectively

Transition	High	Low
(1) Start with D from the top. End with D	1	18
(2) Start with D from the bottom. End with D	0	14
(3) Start without D. End with C at P tags	0	17
(4) Start without D. End with C at I tags	0	3
(5) Start without D. End with C at N tags	1	1
(6) Start with D from the top. End with C at P tags	10	8
(7) Start with D from the top. End with C at I tags	0	0
(8) Start with D from the top. End with C at N tags	0	0
(9) Start with D from the bottom. End with C at P tags	1	3
(10) Start with D from the bottom. End with C at I tags	0	0
(11) Start with D from the bottom. End with C at N tags	0	2

the idea, the communication ended with positive utterances (Nos. 6–9). In most communications with a (6)-like transition, the deficiencies pointed out by investors are solved, and the idea is eventually accepted by both investors and consumers. This means that negative utterances actually improve ideas. Therefore, when transition (6) appears, an idea is expected to be successful.

Fig. 7.8 Examples of a divergence from the bottom and a divergence from the top in the tag transitions

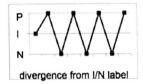

divergence from I/N label

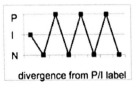

divergence from P/I label

Table 7.7 Example of a communication that corresponds to transition (6)

No.	Player	Utterance
1	Inventor (I)	I propose an idea for reducing grime in pipes by combining plastic pipes and fat splitting in the ozone
2	Investor 1 (N4)	It might be risky to use ozone if people are near the system
3	Inventor (P)	That might be so
4	Investor 1 (N3)	How could you reduce the risks?
5	Inventor (P)	Well, even if people inhaled ozone, they would not get ill right away. Anyway, in my idea the pipes are placed on the ground and then set underground, but the ozone system is only underground So, if any accidents happened, nobody would get hurt because they would be too far away
6	Investor 2 (P)	Do you think that simply placing the ozone system far away from people will make it safe?
7	Inventor (P)	Yes, I do
8	Investor 1 (P)	OK I accept your idea
9	Investor 2 (P)	Me too

However, there were times when transition (6) appeared in communications about ideas that turned out to receive low investments. The rate of each negative tag in communications with transition (6) is shown in Fig. 7.9. The rate of N2 for highly invested ideas was higher than that for lowly invested ones. We take this to mean that inventors obtained acceptance from investors by adding explanations to their original idea. In contrast, the rate of N4 for low-investment ideas was higher than for high-investment ones (Chi-squared $= 16.4$, $p = 0.009 < 0.1$, r (N2) $= 3.41$, r (N4) $= 3.35$). This means that irreversible defects were included in the proposed ideas. Although the inventors tried to fix these defects, the ideas did not ultimately garner much investment.

Transitions in which ideas did not receive a big investment were transitions (1), (2), and (3) in Table 7.6. In transitions (1) and (2), there were rounds of positive/negative utterances and the communication ended with a divergence. Table 7.8 shows an example of communication with transition (1). The first utterance was an idea proposal, which investors then criticized in utterance Nos. 2, 5, and 7. The inventor could not cope well with these criticisms - although he tried with utterance No. 8 – and ultimately failed to obtain acceptance from investors. That was why his idea did not receive a big investment.

In transition (3), there were no positive/negative rounds, and the communication ended with a positive utterance. An example of a communication with transition (3)

Fig. 7.9 Rates of each negative utterance in an example of transition (6)

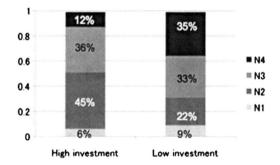

Table 7.8 Example of a communication corresponding to transition (1)

No.	Player	Utterance
1	Inventor (I)	I propose an idea for automatically adding bath salts to a bath by combining a pump with safety valves and a bath
2	Investor 1 (N3)	I would rather put the bath salt in by myself than have it automatically done
3	Investor 2 (P)	Yes, me too!
4	Inventor (N2)	But this system uses a solid bath salt, not a liquid one
5	Investor 1 (N3)	Well, but I enjoy watching the bath salt dissipate after I add it to a bath
6	Inventor (P)	You like watching it, do you?
7	Investor 3 (N2)	Yes. It's fun
8	Inventor (N2)	I'm not sure everybody would agree …

Table 7.9 Example of a communication corresponding to transition (3)

No.	Player	Utterance
1	Inventor (I)	I propose an idea for a dance service combining dancing robots, a partition system, and a 10-min haircut
2	Investor 1 (P)	I see
3	Inventor (I)	Would you invest in this idea?
4	Investor 2 (P)	Well, it sounds interesting
5	Investor 3 (P)	Could we use only the haircut service if we like?
6	Inventor (P)	Yes, you can. In such a case, we would create a different system for the charges

is shown in Table 7.9. Here, the first utterance was by an inventor, who proposed an idea about a dance service with robots after a haircut. Even though investors made positive utterances (Nos. 2 and 4), they did not invest much money. This implies that investors may make positive utterances even if they do not fully accept an idea.

All in all, we can conclude that the type-(6) transition in Table 7.6 contributes to the generation of ideas that receive big investments, especially if the negative comments have an N2 tag. Although ideas that receive negative comments from investors tend to be invested in less, players should be conscious of the overall process of communication.

7.4 Summary: Seven Lessons for Players

In this section, we list seven lessons obtained from the results of our experiments that can be applied to actual workplaces to elevate the level of innovation.

Lesson 1   Be patient. Wait until ideas have been created from combinations of ideas in clusters on the graph, without worrying too much about getting a high score. Further into the game, start using ideas at the niches between clusters of activated ideas on the graph.

Lesson 2   If a player does not mind taking risks to create a hit (and hopefully a high score), try to create ideas at the free space between clusters including activated (used) ideas.

Lesson 3   If a player wants a degree of reliability (hedging the risk of low score), create ideas on existing nodes or lines on the graph.

Lesson 4   If a player cannot wait for clusters to become occupied by activated ideas – i.e., if one prefers to combine ideas in clusters both with and without activated ideas – it is recommended to create an idea on a node connecting these clusters.

Lesson 5   Do not to jump to a new use scene before others are satisfied with thinking and talking on the proposed use scene. That is, be empathetic - continue discussing the current use scene until the time comes to propose your own.

Lesson 6   Be conscious of the overall process of communication, rather than worrying about each comment.

Lesson 7   Encourage yourself and others to criticize others with comments to clarify the details of a proposed idea that is difficult to understand and/or accept. For example, explain why you cannot accept the idea.

References

Nishihara Y, Ohsawa Y (2010) Communication analysis on innovators market game. In: Proceedings on the 11th international symposium on knowledge systems sciences (KSS2010), Xian Jiaotong University

Ohsawa Y, Nishihara Y (2009) Niche of idea activations as source of social creativity. In: Proceedings of the 2009 IEEE international conference on systems, man, and cybernetics (SMC2009), Texas. IEEE Press, Piscataway, pp 1704–1709

Chapter 8
Innovators' Marketplace as Integrated Process: An Industrial Case

The Innovators' Marketplace is a process of innovative thought and communication that utilizes the Innovators' Market Game (IMG) as a core step. In this chapter, we present a practical case where we integrated cycles of the game by using chance discovery (see Chaps. 2 and 3) and created and evaluated scenarios of future policies in a target domain.

Let us here review the double helix (DH) process of chance discovery we introduced in Chapter 3 where (1) object data, such as sales data and Web-posted text relevant to the participants' interests, are visualized as a graph shown to participants, and then (2) subject data, i.e., the records of cognition and thought, such as conversational logs, memos, or eye movements of participants who discussed the graph, are visualized in some way. This visual information is shown to the participants again so that they can acquire a new focus of interest for collecting new data and then return to (1). This process has been remodeled as the Innovators' Marketplace in this chapter, and IMG can be regarded as a tool for organizing conversations with the visual sharing of initial data and the subsequent collection of subject data. The Analogy Game introduced in Chap. 5 is another tool that is integrated into the process, as exemplified by a case we present in Chap. 9.

In this chapter, we present a case in which we applied the process of Innovators' Marketplace to a real business to assist the employees in coming up with innovative new strategies. In order to cope with the complexity of real scenarios, we introduce a tsugological framework as the backbone of thoughts and communications. Users had the freedom to choose tools other than KeyGraph for visualization in (1) or (2) above.

8.1 Innovators' Market Game as a Process Coupled with Tsugology

In the Innovators' Marketplace, IMG has been integrated with the DH process to encourage the externalization of *tsugoes* (defined later in this section) and innovative

Y. Ohsawa and Y. Nishihara, *Innovators' Marketplace*, Understanding Innovation, DOI 10.1007/978-3-642-25480-2_8, © Springer-Verlag Berlin Heidelberg 2012

thoughts and conversations by combining basic pieces of knowledge. This process is composed of the following five steps (see also Fig. 8.1):

Step (1)   Learn essential concepts for the process. We first give a brief lecture on the process and the essential concepts that players should learn in advance. Participants learn the importance of a process-oriented mind (being conscious of the process for discovery, as in Chap. 3, and the lessons presented at the end of Chap. 7, rather than the technical features of the tool for visualization), as well as new concepts such as tsugology.

Step (2)   Determine the tsugological relationships among participants. We recommend that players share and examine the graph visualizing the collected data/documents relevant to the interests of the other players so that they will be aware of their own positions in the market. This will enable them to write, think, and talk about action plans, essential intentions, and constraints (which are the essence of tsugoes). In cases where there is no such data, step (2) should be skipped for the moment and returned to when possible.

Step (3)   Create and visualize basic cards and their correlations. Based on their awareness of their positions and tsugoes within the group, participants use their business-related knowledge to create basic cards and then visualize the relationships among these cards to produce a game board.

Step (4)   Play IMG. Participants play IMG using the basic cards they created and the graph (game board) obtained in step (3).

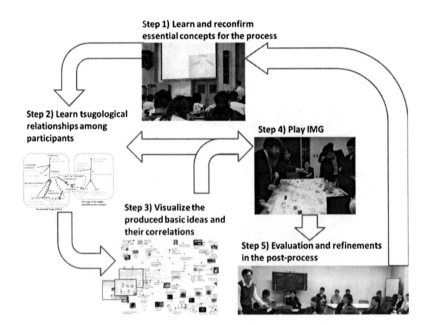

Fig. 8.1 The process of Innovators' Marketplace

Step (5)   Evaluation and refinements in the post-process. The ideas obtained during the game are evaluated on the basis of criteria corresponding to the requirements of the group. Novelty, utility, and reality are typical examples of essential criteria, as noted in Chap. 7. Let us note here briefly that reality means if a particular idea can be realized in realistic conditions, whereas utility means how useful the idea is if realized. This step may be executed just for selecting the best ideas, but it is preferable to actually evaluate the ideas so that they can be double-checked and improved (if necessary) to make them more suitable for actual application in a business. If necessary, step (1) can be repeated to enhance the participants' awareness of constraints, and running the entire process again can lead to the creation of more realistic ideas (we sometimes go through the entire five steps three times or more).

8.2   Learn the Concepts (Step (1)) for Executing Innovators' Marketplace: Tsugology, an Idea Representation Approach for Solving Conflicts and Enhancing Value Creation

Although we invented IMG as a means for facilitating chance discovery while coping with the difficulty of surviving criticisms and conflicts, we still had problems when applying it to real businesses, as noted at the end of Chap. 6. The main issue was that the ideas business people came up with while they played the game were often rejected when they were actually proposed in the participants' companies.

We found that most rejections were the result of two elements: *prior constraints*, which came from previously existing resource limitations (mainly financial or technological), and *posterior constraints*, which came from conflict between the expected result of a created idea and *intentions*, either of one's own or of other stakeholders. In order to circumvent these two elements, we developed what we call a *tsugological approach* for creating realistic strategies. In tsugology, a set of these three factors – the prior and posterior constraints and the intention of self or stakeholder – is called a *tsugo*. We provide a more formal definition of tsugo later.

In human–human communication, a large portion of tsugo tends to be hidden due to the inadequacy of verbally expressed claims in daily life. As a result, humans can come across as unreasonable decision makers, behaving inconsistently with previous actions and utterances. We assume this superficial inconsistency emerges from an incomplete awareness of one's own intentions or constraints. This can cause miscommunication and the loss of trust, which in turn causes difficulties in restarting communications and even the destruction of human relationships. We use tsugology to improve and optimize both the effects and the efficiency of communications and actions in business/politics/etc. by modeling and externalizing stakeholders' tsugoes (Ohsawa 2010; Ohsawa et al. 2010). In this section, we describe tsugology in more detail to clarify its role in the Innovators' Marketplace.

Tsugology is a research focus that deals with *tsugoes*, which are a set of the intention of an individual and constraints that may restrict or accelerate the realization of his/her intention. The word "tsugo," which is Japanese, is a little difficult to translate into other languages. A Japanese-English dictionary provides multiple translations for "tsugo," such as (1) circumstances, (2) convenience, (3) opportunity, (4) reason, (5) arrangement(s), and more. We find it difficult to settle on an English word that precisely matches "tsugo," so let us just say that tsugology aims to establish a method for coping with conflicts between the intentions and constrains of stakeholders and to turn these conflicts into the synergetic creation of values.

An important challenge in tsugology is to urge stakeholders to speak or write about their tsugoes explicitly and to the required extent. This is because incomplete expression can sometimes cause inefficient trackbacks in communication and may force the restarting of a project if the latent conflict is externalized later on. The aim of tsugology is thus to encourage individuals to express tsugoes and to complete a process for detecting violated hidden constraints and solutions for overcoming the violation. Ideally, this will lead to the creation of a feasible plan of action in business.

More formally, a *tsugo* (A) is defined as a set of one's intention (I) underlying an action A, and the constraints restricting/caused by the action. These constraints include prior constraints (Pr, the set of constraints that may restrict A) and posterior constraints (Ps, the constraints resulting from action A, which may restrict other actions – of either the original actor or of others).

For example, an individual might say, "Today, I'm unable to attend the meeting due to a tsugo," followed by no further explanation of the real reason he/she cannot go. Here, we find that the tsugo is just a meaningless word because it does not explain anything about the reason for the absence. If a co-worker were to say, "Mr. X says he is unable to join us today due to his personal tsugo," most of us would probably feel that Mr. X is hiding his real intention (e.g., perhaps he really just likes to go out drinking from early in the evening). Overall, a tsugo should be regarded as structure connecting an action (A) to the actor's intention and two kinds of constraints, of which some essential parts may be consciously or unconsciously hidden. As an example, let us take the action of Mr. X (the actor) leaving the office early as A. Note that the complex expression of the elements of tsugo that follows is to give the reader a detailed understanding of the meaning of tsugoes. The reader is free to skip this section, as it will not create a serious disadvantage when reading the remainder of the book.

- I (Intention): The goal aimed for with action A. For example, the intention of Mr. X's action A may be to drink at a bar.
- Pr (Prior constraints): The set of constraints that may restrict A. Pr includes conditional rules such as $A <- cpr_1, cpr_2, \ldots cpr_m$, and situations $spr_1, spr_2, \ldots spr_m$, where cpr_i may be violated or satisfied by spr_i or by the satisfaction of other constraints. For example, action A above may require the condition cpr_3 "if Mr. X's boss is absent," and this condition will be violated if the situation spr_3

"the boss has returned from her business trip" is true. In general, Pr may start from a small set and grow as the actor notices the actions and events relevant to executing action A.

- Ps (Posterior constraints): The constraints resulting from action A, which may restrict either the actions of the original actor or of others. That is, a posterior constraint of action A is a situation caused by A that may become a prior constraint of other actions. For example, Mr. X's action A to leave the office early may raise a posterior constraint cps (which is really a situation spr') that he is absent, violating the prior constraint of the others, i.e., "We can only conduct the budget plan meeting (the intended action) if everybody is here."

Note that a posterior constraint of an action can sometimes create a prior constraint. For example, the situation caused by action A – i.e., the posterior constraint of A ("Mr. X is absent") and its inconsistency with the tsugo of the budget committee – may cause Mr. X to remember the budget plan meeting and notice the previously unnoticed condition ("Mr. X can leave the office if he does not have a meeting") for going out, i.e., for action A. Then, the prior constraint of A will be extended with two additional constraints, cpr_4 and spr (as in the bottom of Fig. 8.2), which externalizes a latent inconsistency.

A noteworthy point is that the posterior constraints or the created prior constraints will not be included in the frame of an individual's awareness: essentially, the effect of the posterior constraints on other tsugoes is not noticed. I, Pr, and Ps represent the world of actions and affected events filtered by the actor's awareness, and only a part, not the whole, of the real world can be expressed. This double-filter system makes communicated tsugoes incomplete. The importance of externalizing the set $\{A, I, Pr, Ps\}$ might be easier to understand if we think of two specific targets, e.g., negotiations and design communications.

Negotiations   A group meeting where a consensus to take a certain action is reached is a target of tsugology. A negotiation can be difficult because it can sometimes break down into a dispute, as in cases where participants are required to reach a consensus but have intentions and constraints that are difficult to satisfy simultaneously. Adding to the general atmosphere of frustration in cases like this, it can often appear that a consensus has been reached but participants might have ignored a prior constraint Pr, which may halt the action, or might have ignored the possibility of bothering others by a posterior constraint Ps, or might have ignored an intention I of latent stakeholders. The introduction of tsugology to a negotiation will clarify the focus of conflicts and improve the efficiency of decision making among groups of people.

The design of products and services   If an essential part of the tsugoes of important stakeholders is hidden, the resulting miscommunication may lead to conflicts after days, weeks, or even years. Products and services made without externalizing the customers' intentions and constraints tend to turn out in an unsatisfactory way. Taking careful note of the tsugoes of customers/users via well-coordinated

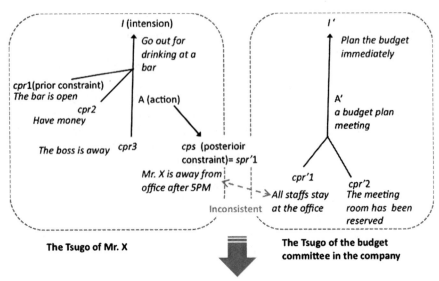

The Tsugo of Mr. X

The Tsugo of the budget
committee in the company

The section should change the constraint cpr'1 and decide to change the rule (start the meeting without Mr. X), or call Mr. X to have him recollect the budget plan meeting.

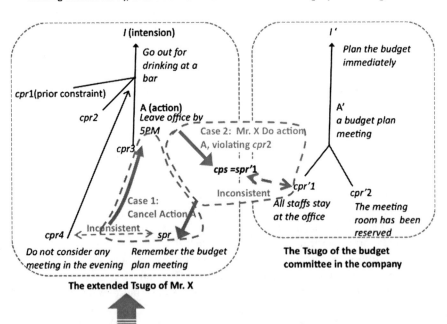

The budget committee called Mr. X to have him recollect the budget plan meeting, and Mr. X noticed there has been prior constraints he did not consider so far.

Fig. 8.2 The tsugoes of Mr. X and the budget committee of his company

questions and communications is essential for creating sustained value. By highlighting important tsugoes and considering their mutual influences at suitable moments, we can expect to come up with highly satisfactory products and services.

Hereafter, we take a closer look at the second target. Methods for identifying and considering the requirements of customers/users have previously been studied in the domain of requirement acquisition (RA), where the main focus has been on retrieving the purposes (corresponding to "intentions" above), methods, and conditions ("actions" and "constraints" above) necessary to meet consumer demand (see e.g. Carrol 2000; Goldratt 1987; Kushiro and Ohsawa 2006). Kushiro and Ohsawa developed an RA method in which the reasons for both accepting and rejecting possible strategies for meeting a customer's requirement are discussed by considering the intentions, actions, and constraints of the stakeholders, including customers and designers. Tests of this method showed that it improved the efficiency of both the RA and the quality of products (Kushiro and Ohsawa 2006). It works like this: designers accept a strategy if it corresponds to the statements about actions and to the possibility of satisfying prior constraints, whereas discussion about why designers should reject a possibility may lead to the externalization of latent posterior constraints. For example, the question "Why do you want the bicycle spokes to be made out of stainless steel?" may cause the user to respond, "Because stainless steel spokes meet the condition tied to my long commute to work (prior constraint)." In contrast, the question "Why don't we make the bicycle spokes with aluminum?" may induce the response "If we did, users who carry heavy bags every day would probably break the wheel within a month," thereby externalizing the possibility of conflict between the bicycle design and the intention of specific users (posterior constraint).

As the above examples show, the externalization of tsugoes via verbal communication plays an essential role in RA. The more completely one grasps a customer's tsugo, the more feasible and satisfactory the resulting design is likely to be. For the business case presented below, we encouraged participants to focus their consideration on one another's tsugoes throughout the entire process of Innovators' Marketplace. We will discuss the tsugological approach in more detail in the case we present in Chap. 9.

8.3 IMG for Creating Products/Services and Visions (for Business in Company A)

8.3.1 The Participants and Basic Cards

The core business of company A is designing/producing printed materials. They also offer services extending from their printing technologies, such as producing RFID tags on demand, creating postcards for individual customers at high speed for a low cost, etc. Recently, this company wanted to come up with some new ideas for their business by combining ideas/knowledge from both in/outside themselves.

After our lecture on tsugology and process-consciousness in the context of Innovators' Marketplace, several individuals from this company made 80 basic cards, about half of which contained ideas/knowledge from inside the company and half of which were from outside. They played IMG three times, plus one warm-up game. Here, we give an overview of the three games. The players were recruited from multiple sections of the company, including sales promotion, marketing development, business planning, technology promotion, and the sales force. The number of players ranged from six to ten for all games. It would have made sense to include players from outside of the company given their particular desire (ideas/knowledge from inside/outside), but we restricted play to employees of the company because important ideas for new products should not be revealed to others until they start dealing with the created products/services in real business scenarios. Collecting players from multiple sections who shared the above desire was the best we could do in terms of customizing their gaming plan.

Business workers, as far as they survive what ever section they may work in, are constantly embracing hidden contexts they acquire in the course of their business experiences, and these unconscious contexts have a big effect on their product planning and design, service provision, etc. In company A, where up-to-date technologies and business knowledge are known by everybody and used on a daily basis, it is rather a difficult task to verbalize tacit dimensions of knowledge. In order to create strategic scenarios for new business by combining pieces of knowledge with the latent feeling of common contexts among players, they first needed to choose the most suitable visualization tool. In this case, they did not choose KeyGraph because its edges are said to be an over-externalization of hidden relationships among technologies.

Here, the relevance among the basic cards was visualized in a map, as shown in Figs. 8.3–8.5. The letters beside each node correspond to the title of each basic card. The visualization tool chosen here was based on the PSI algorithm (Bai et al. 2009), summarized below. Note: This case was exceptional only in that KeyGraph was replaced with another tool.

8.3.2 Summary of PSI-Based Visualization of Positions of Basic Cards

(1) Participants classify basic cards into two groups intuitively. For company A, the cards were classified on the criterion of whether or not each card could contribute to innovation in their business domain. Intuitions are expected to reflect their tacit knowledge acquired from experience.

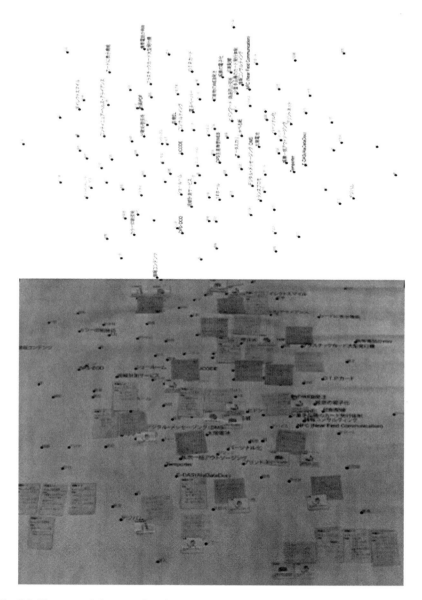

Fig. 8.3 The map of the game board (*upper*), embedded with colored basic cards and white requirement cards (*lower*). The final situation of Game 1 (B to B + C) was discussed. The notes are written in Japanese, so please just observe the distribution of cards

(2) Polynomial Semantic Indexing (PSI) is used as a reinforcement learning method to learn the relevance of each pair of words included in the basic cards, based on the subjects' classification of the cards in (1).

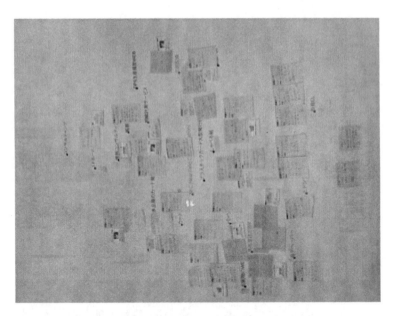

Fig. 8.4 The final situation of Game 2 (B to B) was discussed

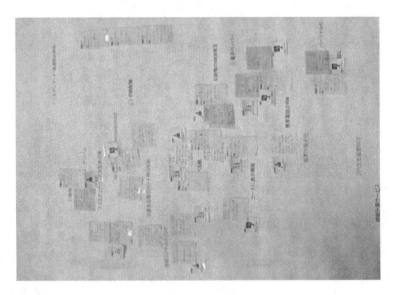

Fig. 8.5 Game 3 (B to C)

(3) Reflect the word-to-word relevance computed in (2) to card-to-card similarities, and visualize the positions of cards by nodes so that similar cards are placed close together on the map.

Briefly, this method combines two kinds of information: (a) the similarity of cards via the included words and (b) the underlying interests of subjects that relate to the words from behind the superficial expressions in the text of basic cards. Readers may notice that the combination of Innovators' Market Game (IMG) and Analogy Game (AG), to be exemplified in the next chapter, also reflect both (a) and (b); in fact, the whole point of AG is to collect the information of (b). However, if the players do not have enough time to play AG, simply classifying basic cards into two groups in a couple of minutes for the PSI-based visualization can be an efficient alternative, although the simplicity may cause some of the information to be missed.

8.3.3   To B, C, or B + C

One of our primary goals with IM for company A was to clarify their business vision. Here, the participants had to decide whether they should continue their services only for business people (Business to Business, or B to B) or expand to include final consumers in their business target (Business to Consumers, or B to C). In order to satisfy this aim, we created different sets of consumer sub-role cards (see Chap. 6 to review sub-role cards). When participants were inventing ideas for B to B, the consumer sub-role cards included "credit card company," "supermarket," etc., which represented customers who buy inventors' ideas for business use, and when they were inventing ideas for B to C, the consumer sub-role cards included "elderly people," "students," etc., which represented customers who ultimately consume the provided products/services. Here, we changed the gaming framework slightly, as follows.

- Game 1: B to B + C (consumer sub-roles were taken arbitrarily, including both business people/companies and end consumers)
- Game 2: B to B (consumer sub-roles included only businesses, because participants did not have any significant conflicts in Game 1; see Sect. 8.4)
- Game 3: B to C (consumer sub-roles included only end consumers, for the purpose of comparison with Game 2)

These changes reflected our identification of participants' sense of their own positions in the market in such a way as to visualize the human tsugo network (HTN), as discussed in the next section.

In addition, we introduced *requirement cards* here as a new element. In order to explicitly express the opinions of consumers, we had them write important requirements on white sticky labels (white has never been the color of any inventors) while reading them out. Although there are differences in the number of created ideas (colored labels) in Figs. 8.3–8.5, the positions of the requirement cards are more important in terms of evaluating the quality of the discussion. Some requirement cards are located in areas isolated from nodes (i.e., basic cards) in the map of the game board in Fig. 8.3, while in Figs. 8.4 and 8.5 the requirement cards are put in areas between the nodes. This means that the consumers gradually learned via the requirements that they could deduce possible links to the latent context underlying the empty space surrounded by basic cards.

8.4 An Additional Use of Tsugology: Visualization of Human Tsugo Network (HTN in Step (2))

In order to determine the relative positions of the players, here we introduced another way to use tsugology: visualizing the human tsugo network (HTN). An HTN is a network representing interactions among the intentions and constraints of stakeholders (an example is shown in Fig. 8.2). We can visualize a rough HTN from a discourse log based on the following three assumptions:

(1) The action (which can be an utterance) of person X co-occurs with the intention of X.
(2) The pre-constraint of X, for an action of X, occurred before the action.
(3) The action of X is followed by X's post-constraint on other actions (of X him/herself or other people).

Here, an important point is that the intention and the constraints of an action are addressed to the actor – i.e., human X, who performs the action – rather than to the action itself. Strictly speaking, this point is inconsistent with the formal definition of tsugoes in Sect. 8.2, where tsugoes were defined as the attributes of an action. However, the three assumptions above are suitable for positioning humans rather than actions, considering that, in our experience at least, an individual's intention and constraints do not change rapidly. The overview of the procedure for visualizing an HTN is as follows.

Step (1)   Produce a dataset of utterances where each line includes one utterance.
Step (2)   Replace all utterances (i.e., all lines) by person X with X_{int}.
Step (3)   To each line, insert Y_{pre}, where Y is the person whose utterance was just after the utterance in the line. Also, insert Z_{pst}, where Z is the person whose utterance was just before the utterance in the line.
Step (4)   To each line, insert the content of the next line (to take into account the lingering of one utterance to two or more moments after).

In the obtained HTN, X_{int} means the intention of X, X_{pst} means the post constraint (i.e., the effect of X on other participants' thoughts and utterances), and X_{pre} means the prior constraint (i.e., the effect that X receives from others). For example, suppose four people are playing IMG, and X is making a presentation about his idea while the others are trying to determine the quality.

Mr. X: This is a speaking helmet. What do you think?
Mr. Y: Maybe I like it, but I'm a bit confused...
Ms. Z: This idea looks interesting. How much is it?
Mr. X: How much can you pay?

Ms. Z: I'll pay two Monkeys. What do you say?
Mr. X: Hmmm. . . I really couldn't go lower than three Monkeys.
Mr. Y: That's too expensive!
    Especially since it wouldn't even work if the rescue team was far way!
Ms. Z: That's true. Why don't you implement a light as well?
Mr. X: That's not a bad idea. A speaking light on a helmet!
Mr. U: Speaking light. . . What if it's in the daytime?
Mr. X: Daytime? No problem.
Mr. U: Why not?
Mr. X: It's not so cold, so a man wouldn't have to worry as much.
Mr. Y: What if it's a woman? She might be attacked . . .
Ms. Z: I think daytime is just as dangerous as night.

In step (1), we obtain the second column in Eq. (8.1), as framed by the bold line. In Step (2) and (3), the first three items in each line as in the thinner frame are inserted. Finally, in step (4), we include the last three items in each line to represent lingering effect of each utterance to its following utterance.

$$D_{tsugo} =$$

X_{pre}					
Y_{pre}	X_{int}				
Z_{pre}	Y_{int}	X_{pst}			
X_{pre}	Z_{int}	Y_{pst}	X_{pre}		
Z_{pre}	X_{int}	Z_{pst}	Y_{pre}	X_{int}	
X_{pre}	Z_{int}	X_{pst}	Z_{pre}	Y_{int}	X_{pst}
Y_{pre}	X_{int}	Z_{pst}	X_{pre}	Z_{int}	Y_{pst}
Z_{pre}	Y_{int}	X_{pst}	Z_{pre}	X_{int}	Z_{pst}
X_{pre}	Z_{int}	Y_{pst}	X_{pre}	Z_{int}	X_{pst}
U_{pre}	X_{int}	Z_{pst}	Y_{pre}	X_{int}	Z_{pst}
X_{pre}	U_{int}	X_{pst}	Z_{pre}	Y_{int}	X_{pst}
U_{pre}	X_{int}	U_{pst}	X_{pre}	Z_{int}	Y_{pst}
X_{pre}	U_{int}	X_{pst}	U_{pre}	X_{int}	Z_{pst}
Y_{pre}	X_{int}	U_{pst}	X_{pre}	U_{int}	X_{pst}
Z_{pre}	Y_{int}	X_{pst}	U_{pre}	X_{int}	U_{pst}
	Z_{int}	Y_{pst}	X_{pre}	U_{int}	X_{pst}
		Z_{pst}	Y_{pre}	X_{int}	U_{pst}
			Z_{pre}	Y_{int}	X_{pst}
				Z_{int}	Y_{pst}
					Z_{pst}

$$(8.1)$$

We obtain Fig. 8.6 by applying KeyGraph to D_{tsugo}. X_{int} is linked to X_{pst} and X_{pre}, which means that the intention of Mr. X is strongly constrained by his own prior constraint and also places a posterior constraint on others, as in X_{pst}. The diffused constraint X_{pst} affects Ms. Z, as the link to Z_{pre} shows.

Fig. 8.6 The HTN obtained
for the sample discourse

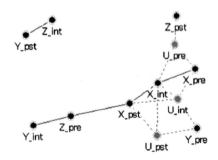

Actually, Ms. Z listened carefully to Mr. X and made careful comments evaluating his ideas, and she also listened to Mr. Y and was affected by his intention, as the link from Y_{int} to Z_{pre} shows. In contrast, it looks like Mr. Y influences Ms. Z rather than being influenced by others. In fact, if we look at the discourse, it appears that Mr. Y spoke as soon as a thought popped into his head. Mr. U is at an interesting position: Mr. U spoke only twice, but he introduced a new viewpoint: that it is pointless to wear a speaking helmet with a light in the daytime. The log showed that Mr. X could not provide a satisfactory response to this criticism, suggesting that perhaps he should continue thinking of ways to improve his idea. This conflict between Mr. X and Mr. U is shown via the link between X_{pst} and U_{pst}, which means that Mr. X and Mr. U are exerting their influence on each other rather than trying to satisfy each other's requirements.

Now, let us return to company A. Figure 8.7 shows the HTNs for the conversations in Game 1 (upper) and Game 2 (lower). In Game 2, we used only end-consumer sub-role cards for the B to B environment because we noticed that the participants were not eager to join discussions unless the focus was on dealing with business people.

On the basis of the amount of money each inventor had at the end of the game, inventor C ranked first, inventor A was second, and inventor B was third. If we compare this result with the upper part of Fig. 8.7, we can hypothesize that the more actively an inventor communicates with a consumer whose sub-role is obvious, the more highly evaluated the inventor will be. The lower part of Fig. 8.7 shows the results for Game 2, where inventor B ranked first, inventor C was second, and inventor A was third. Although inventor A may seem central in Fig. 8.7 (lower), a further investigation of his communication clarifies the reason for his low rank. That is, if we look at the consumers' ranking, the hospital was first, the convenience store was second, and the airline was third; of these, inventor B is linked to the convenience store whereas inventor A is linked to the government, whose rank was actually lower than the top four. This demonstrates that choosing a promising communication partner is an effective approach to innovation, especially when creating useful (not just novel) ideas is desired.

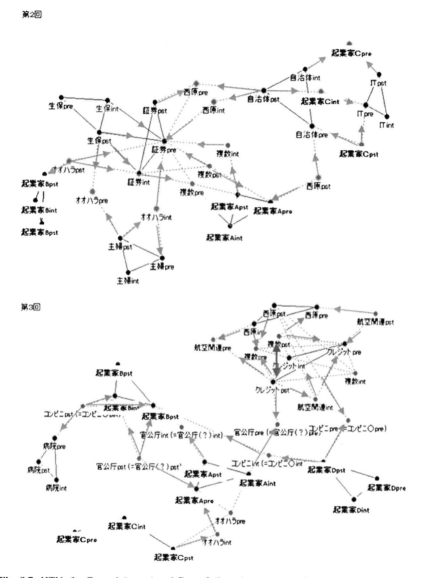

Fig. 8.7 HTNs for Game 1 (*upper*) and Game 2 (*lower*) at company A

HTN also provides an important lesson about communication for innovation. As evident in Fig. 8.6, the adjacent positioning of X_{pst} and U_{pst} indicates a conflict between Mr. X and Mr. U, where neither is helping to solve the other's problem. This deadlock might look bad, but actually it leads to the awareness of essential problems. In the case of the sample conversation above, after hard thinking triggered by the conflict, Mr. X is likely to invent an effective tool for overcoming the problem presented by Mr. U (saving lives in the daytime): perhaps a supersonic device to be put on the helmet. In the case of the lower part of Fig. 8.7, the conflict is between the credit card firm and multiple others. A portion of their conversation is shown below.

Credit card firm to inventor: If you create something by combining the goggle and the towel, the interestingness and the high functionality of both will attract consumers.
Multiple: Huh. . .?
Credit card firm: I don't have much money to invest, however.
Inventor: That's true, you have too little money to pay me to make something interesting.
Credit card firm: Oh, that's too bad. . .

The expression of negative feeling ("Huh. . .?") by multiple participants is meant to urge the consumer positioned as a staff member of a credit card firm to say something more meaningful, thereby enabling the inventor to improve his idea. We cannot always say good ideas occur between such conflicting participants. However, this kind of conflict involves other participants into an air where conflicts are accepted. This can help improve the process of innovative communications. As we discussed in Chap. 7, in successful cases, a conversation will evolve into a negotiation between inventors and consumers that improves the inventors' ideas, making them more suitable for the demands of consumers. In other words, negotiations sometimes give birth to solutions with a high business value. The ideas born in Game 2 had the highest evaluations of ideas in all three games as a direct result of this. A short portion of the discussion in Game 2 is shown below as an example.

Inventor A: I propose a new product called an "alerting PTP sheet." This is a press through package, or PTP, that notifies the patient if it is not the correct time to take the medicine or not the right quantity of medicine. The PTP has an embedded circuit which, if the package breaks unexpectedly, switches on an alert voice that says something such as "Stop! This medicine is for just after breakfast."
Consumer B: Good idea! But what if the patient takes the medicine at the correct time?
Inventor A: Hmmm. . . The switch doesn't turn on the PTP sheet is used in a correct way. . . What do you think?
Consumer C: Does this mean that the circuit is not cut off if the tablet is peeled off correctly? I'm a little confused. . .
Inventor B: Let me propose an improvement. The number of pills, and the time to ingest them, are transmitted from the sheet to a wireless service terminal in the house, where all decisions are made by artificial intelligence!

This conversation gave birth to the alerting PTP sheet, which was the idea that ranked highest in Game 2. After negative utterances (criticisms) were made during the game, the proposed solutions were evaluated by all participants after the game and the ones that were evaluated as the best were chosen as candidate products or services to be commercialized. Such criticism contributing to improvements was not evident in Game 1; the HTN in the upper part of Fig. 8.7 does not contain any conflict among posterior constraints. In order to encourage players to be more frank, we chose to focus on the players' consideration of B to B strategies in Game 2.

In other instances of HTN we have tested so far, conflict points depicted by the adjacent allocation of two stakeholders were relevant to creative problem-solving and the quality of ideas improved. The same holds true with the examples presented in this book: enjoying the game is significant, because when criticisms and conflicts arise in normal meetings they usually discourage participants from continuing to speak. If it is a game and participants know the criticisms are just a part of playing, the criticisms can actually increase their motivation to speak.

8.5   Step (5): The Evaluation Phase

We evaluated the ideas obtained from the three games (See Table 8.1). In terms of quantity, Game 1 had the best results: 18 ideas emerged, compared to 14 and 13 in Games 2 and 3, respectively. Game 1 might seem to be the most successful if we just take quantity into account. However, when we looked at idea quality, the ranking was different. For this evaluation, the ideas of all three games were shuffled to ensure blind judging and referees evaluated (1) reality, (2) novelty, (3) utility, and (4) interestingness, without being biased by knowing the gaming conditions. Eleven referees evaluated the quality of ideas using these criteria with a worst to best (1–4) scale. Here, we present the idea with the highest score, based on the average of the scores given by all referees on criteria (1)–(4), for each game. Note that the basic technologies combined had been already developed.

The best idea from Game 1 (reality: 2.7, novelty: 2.4, utility: 2.0, interestingness: 2.1 (average)): *An advertisement poster that can be affixed to walls. Easy to add or detach if required*, by combining

• A Web system for ordering printed materials
• A puzzle game in which children stick pieces to a wall and try to make interesting shapes

The best idea from Game 2 (reality: 2.0, novelty: 3.0, utility: 2.5, interestingness: 2.8): *A medicine tablet with a function to alert patients if they try to take the medicine at the wrong time*, by combining

• Technology for embedding an integrated circuit by extending printing technology (in the surface of a tablet)
• Speaking paper

The best idea from Game 3 (reality: 1.6, novelty: 2.6, utility: 2.0, interestingness: 2.8): *Real-time presentation of uttered words on a sheet of paper to assist the elderly or others with hearing difficulties to hear conversations*, by combining

Table 8.1 Ideas created in each game

The role cards	No. of idea	Combined basic cards		Reality	Novelty	Utility	Interestingness	Sum
First game B & C (business and final consumers both included)	1~7							
	8	Web system for ordering printed materials, and Puzzle game: children stick pieces on the wall and try to make interesting shapes	An advertisement poster, which can be stuck on the wall. Easy to add or detach if required	2.7	2.4	2	2.1	9.2
	9~14	Omitted						
	15	R/W by using cellular, and information consulting	Data on the personal history of purchase, and recommendation messages will be sent in	2.8	2.1	2.3	1.75	8.95
	16~18	Omitted						
	Average			2.1	1.8	1.7	1.6	7.2
	Std dev			0.61	0.38	0.40	0.23	1.12

Second game all B (business)							
1			2.8	2.9	1.8	2.3	7.2
2	Speaking paper, sunshine power generator, and foldable helmet	Speaking helmet, which announces the fatal situation if the person lost consciousness and cannot speak	2.4	2.9	2.1	2.8	10.2
3	Omitted						
4			3.3	1.8	3.1	1.8	10
5			2.1	2.3	2.8	2.5	9.7
6	Embedding an integrated circuit by extending printing technology (in the surface of tablet), and speaking paper	A tablet of medicine with the function to alert a patient taking at a wrong time, by combining	2	3	2.5	2.8	10.3
7	Omitted						
8~14	Omitted		2.1	2.9	2.1	2.5	9.6
Average			2.1	2.3	2.1	1.9	8.4
Std dev			0.52	0.43	0.52	0.32	1.79

(continued)

Table 8.1 (continued)

The role cards	No. of idea	Combined basic cards		Reality	Novelty	Utility	Interestingness	Sum
Third game all C (final consumers)	1			3.1	1.6	2.3	1.6	8.6
	2	Omitted		1.5	2.8	1.6	2.1	8
	3							
	4~7	Omitted						
	8	Information personalization, and exhibition room of the nature	Creating a customized homework, for each children, to investigate the relation of the nature and the daily life	2.8	2.1	1.8	2.3	9
	9~12	Omitted						
	13	Speaking paper, and paper with the function to present letters, on the electronic signal sent in	Real-time presentation of uttered words on a sheet of paper, for olding old people having difficulty in hearing conversation	1.6	2.6	2	2.8	9
	Average			1.9	2.2	1.9	2.1	8.1
	Std dev			0.53	0.40	0.34	0.38	0.75

- Speaking paper
- Paper that can present letters on the basis of received electronic signals

The highest ranked idea obtained in Game 2 beat out those in the other two games to win the highest score. According to t-testing, the ideas in Game 2 turned out to be significantly of higher score than Game 1 ($p < 0.05$). When we looked at the average scores for the four criteria, we found that Game 2 scored best for novelty, utility, and interestingness. Game 2 was different from the others in that the consumer sub-role cards belonged to B (Business), which leads us to conclude that the basic attitude toward the B to B strategy is a good choice for the continued creation of profitable business ideas for company A.

Let us briefly note here that, in Game 2, the evaluated scores for the consumer presentations were ranked housekeeper (first), insurance company (second), software developer (third), and local government (fourth), whereas the average score of ideas the consumers bought were ranked housekeeper (first), insurance company (second), information technologies (third), stock brokerage (fourth), and local government (fifth). The relationship between these two scores implies that accountability is an important factor in business success. That is, in order to determine if a product or service will be popular in the marketplace, it is essential to listen to consumers talk about how the product/service affects their lives, in addition to considering the frequency of past purchases.

References

Bai B, Weston J, Grangier D, Collobert R, Sadamasa K, Qi Y, Cortes C, Mohri M (2009) Polynomial semantic indexing. Adv Neural Inf Process Syst 22:64–72

Carrol JM (2000) Making use: scenario-based design of human-computer interactions. MIT press, Cambridge

Goldratt EM (1987) Essays on the theory of constraints. North River, Great Barrington

Kushiro N, Ohsawa Y (2006) A scenario acquisition method with multi-dimensional hearing and hierarchical accommodation process. N Math Nat Comput 2(1):101–113

Ohsawa Y (2010) Tsugology: structuring of intentions and constraints for innovative communication (as plenary lecture). In: Proceedings of the 11th international symposium on knowledge and systems sciences, Xian Jiaotong University, Xian, China, October, 2010

Ohsawa Y, Nishihara Y, Nakamura J, Kushiro N, Nitta K (2010) Tsugology for revealing intentions and constraints. In: Proceedings of the IEEE Conference Systems, Man, and Cybernetics, Istanbul, October 2010

Chapter 9
Application Case: Policies for Long-Lasting Safety of Nuclear Power Plants

9.1 IMG Paired with Analogy Game and Reinforced by Tsugology: A Case in Policy Making Directed at Aging Nuclear Power Plants

In the last chapter, we defined the Innovators' Marketplace as a process of innovative thought and communications that uses the Innovators Market Game (IMG) as a core step. In this chapter, IMG and the Analogy Game (AG) are regarded as tools integrated into the Innovators' Marketplace. AG is included here because it enables participants to reflect on subject data to conceptualize essential goals for technicians at nuclear power plants. The framework of tsugology is used here as the backbone of idea representation. The case we present demonstrates how reflecting on participants' consciousness of tsugoes during the Innovators' Marketplace process has a positive effect on the quality of the ideas obtained.

Before we go into details, let us briefly summarize the process. In the initial phase, participants proposed technologies/actions to solve the aging problem and discussed the relevant tsugoes of stakeholders. Meanwhile, we facilitators encouraged participants to externalize the tsugoes (the intentions and constraints) underlying the proposed technologies.

Thirty six basic cards describing the proposed ideas and relevant tsugoes were created. With their awareness of tsugoes thus enhanced, we had the participants, who represented the stakeholders, play the Analogy Game (AG), where the titles of basic cards were manually arranged/rearranged on a display. Then, we used KeyGraph to visualize the players' touching/moving behaviors in AG, which we expected to reflect the latent interests of the players. This graph was used as the IMG game board. Finally, participants started the actual IMG process and created, discussed, and revised ideas to fit the desires/requirements of consumers (called users in this case). Some of the ideas that were evaluated as highly original, highly in demand, and highly realistic came to be integrated and are being embodied in a new national project in Japan.

Y. Ohsawa and Y. Nishihara, *Innovators' Marketplace*, Understanding Innovation,   149
DOI 10.1007/978-3-642-25480-2_9, © Springer-Verlag Berlin Heidelberg 2012

9.2   The Five-Step Process

AG and IMG were integrated to encourage the externalization of tsugoes, innovative thought, and conversations to obtain satisfactory concepts. In this case, the process was composed of the following five steps, which correspond to the chart in Fig. 8.1 in the previous chapter. These steps will be discussed in more detail in later sections.

Step (1)   Learn essential concepts for the process. We gave a lecture and sent messages (e-mails just for introduction) about the process and the essential concepts the players should learn in advance.

Step (2)   Learn the tsugological relationships of participants. Participants shared and looked at a graph visualizing the collected data relevant to the target domain to become aware of their own positions in the society. Then, they started communicating action plan proposals to extract the essential concepts for producing basic cards of IMG. As we expected, because they understood the tsugoes, they were able to write, think, and talk about action plans and essential intentions and constraints.

Step (3)   Visualize the produced basic cards and their correlations. Based on their awareness of the positions and tsugoes in the group, participants created 36 basic cards on which they wrote the intention and constraints (i.e., the tsugo) of each participant. Next, via the playing behavior from the Analogy Game, the participants' interests underlying the basic cards were externalized and the correlations among basic cards were visualized.

Step (4)   Play IMG. Participants played IMG using the basic cards and the new graph (game board) obtained in step (3).

Step (5)   Evaluation and refinements in the post-process. The ideas obtained in IMG were evaluated on the basis of criteria corresponding to the requirements of the group. Novelty, utility, and reality were the core criteria, and reflected to the refinement of the ideas.

In the following sections, we discuss the process of step (2) in detail. We skip step (1) because its fundamental concepts are similar to those presented in Chap. 8. We will also give a summary of step (5), which took quite a long time to perform in this case for the refinement of ideas. It is noteworthy that the process we present here led to the initiation of a new project overseen by the government of Japan, in part due to our sending them our results and also to the enormous social and safety implications of the 2011 Tohoku earthquake and tsunami.

9.3   Step (2): Visualize Words in Relevant Documents and Start Discussing Actions and Tsugoes

We called for participants from stakeholder organizations – e.g., the government, electric power companies, manufacturers of atomic reactors and components,

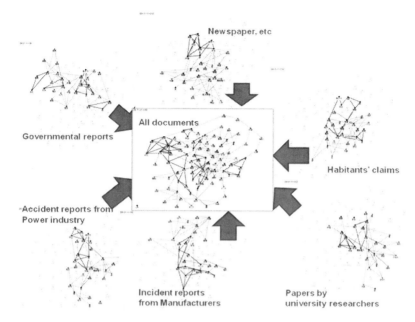

Fig. 9.1 Graphs obtained from documents written by stakeholders

academic societies, and universities – who are involved in the problem of aging nuclear power plants. Ten participants joined the process.

We initially used KeyGraph to visualize the co-occurrence of words in 30 reports (five each from the government, power companies, manufacturers, local inhabitants, the mass media, and universities) related to major accidents at nuclear power plants in Japan (Figs. 9.1–9.8). The shortest report was about 2 pages, but half of them ranged from 30–50 pages. The graphs were printed on transparent sheets so that participants could compare them easily. Participants gathered in a room to look at the graphs and take note of the position of each stakeholder's interest. For example, the government reports about the accident at the Mihama plant referred to corrosions and deterioration caused by the long-lasting use of plants, and were focused on the inspection of pipe wall thinning (Fig. 9.3). Manufacturers (Fig. 9.4), in contrast, are more concerned about their firms' quality control activities for avoiding accidents. University researchers (Fig. 9.5) seemed to be interested in the nature of the metal used in the pipelines and also in methods for evaluating the safety and security of nuclear power plants. The mass media (Fig. 9.6) wrote about the more sensational events such as the death of workers in nuclear power plants resulting from accidents, and also about re-opening dates, which are probably of interest to the average citizen. Inhabitants who live near the atomic plants appear to already have learned a lot about plant management and are interested in technical methods of quality management, e.g., checklists for maintaining the safety of the plant (Fig. 9.7). Finally, the power industry, who are legally of the principal responsibility for nuclear crisis at power plants, are focused on the emergence of extraordinary events relevant

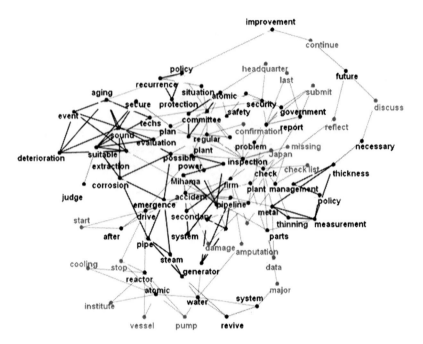

Fig. 9.2 Graph obtained for all documents (all the incident reports we collected). These words were originally in Japanese but here have been translated into English

Fig. 9.3 Graph obtained from government reports

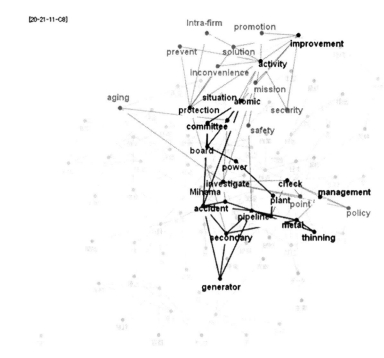

Fig. 9.4 Graph obtained from reports published by reactor manufacturers

to the steam system and to secondary systems that are technically separate from the overall power plant system. Note that we're dealing with aging of nuclear power plants in general (this project was run, as stated, before the crisis at Fukushima Daiichi).

Participants then started sharing their ideas for the long-lasting and safe use of nuclear power plants. A part of this discussion involved identifying their *tsugoes* by filling in a "tsugo form" composed of blanks corresponding to the following items:

- An idea of an *action*
- The *intention* (what effect the action is hoped to have)
- The *prior constraint* (the situation that may restrict/encourage the actions)
- The *posterior constraint* (the effect of the action that may restrict/encourage one's own or other's actions in business or daily life)

The participants did not always fill in all of the blanks. However, it was useful for them to at least try to fill them in because it made the participants aware of the items and enabled them to discuss the underlying intentions and constraints, and also the relationships among different stakeholders' tsugoes.

One hour after starting (early half of step (2)), words in the spoken utterances were transferred into text and the co-relevance of individual words was visualized

[19-21-11-C12]

Fig. 9.5 Graph obtained from scientific papers written by university researchers

[20-21-11-C13]

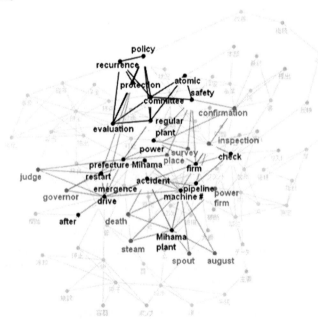

Fig. 9.6 Graph obtained from mass media documents (newspapers, etc.)

[20-21-11-C10]

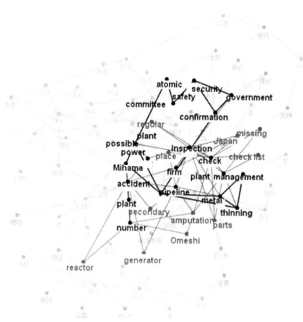

Fig. 9.7 Graph obtained from Web pages written/edited by inhabitants who live near nuclear power plants

by KeyGraph (Fig. 9.9). The links here show the co-occurrence of words in the same utterances. It is apparent from this graph that the participants noticed their own considerations, such as *"mining data reflecting uncertainty in the mind of workers such as plant inspectors," "externalizing hidden concepts of inhabitants living close to plants,"* etc., that corresponded to the word connections in Fig. 9.9. This enabled them to identify valuable scenarios on which they should focus their conversation.

As they continued their discussion with the awareness of specific considerations, the participants began proposing new actions by continuing to fill in the tsugo forms. We extracted action proposals and corresponding tsugoes from these forms and also from the conversational log (text form). In Table 9.1, we show the number of words corresponding to the proposals (1) and the underlying intentions (2) and constraints (3) among those that appeared on the graph shown in Fig. 9.9. Among these words, we also counted the number of words that appeared again in the discussion in the latter half of step (1) (i.e., after showing participants the graph in Fig. 9.9) as an indicator of the extent to which the proposals, the intentions, and the constraints mentioned earlier affected the later conversation.

In Table 9.1, although we see a tendency of words in the early communication (the first hour) to reflect the actions/technologies/research topics proposed in the later hour, the intentions and constraints behind these actions were seldom reflected in the later conversations. That is, oral conversation emphasized the participants'

[20-21-11-C13]

Fig. 9.8 Graph obtained from power industry Web pages

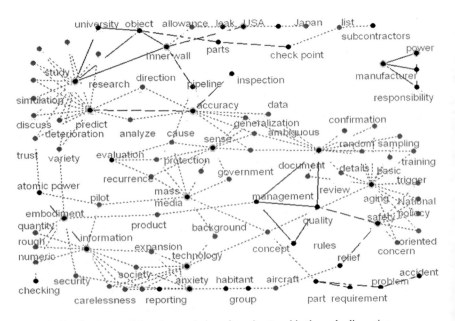

Fig. 9.9 KeyGraph visualizing the correlation of words uttered in the early discussion

Table 9.1 The number of words in the (1) proposals, (2) intentions, and (3) constraints that appeared in the KeyGraph graph used in the earlier half of the conversation, and the number of these words that appeared in the later hour of conversation

	(1) Words in the proposals	(2) Words in the intentions behind the proposed actions	(3) Words in the constraints behind the proposed actions
Total number in Fig. 9.9	41	13	4
No. of words in step (2), after showing Fig. 9.9	27 (66% of the total)	1 (7.7%)	1 (25%)

interest in proposed actions, and this effect was reinforced by the visualization of the discourse, which is regarded as metacognition. However, participants tended to ignore the essence of tsugoes – the participants' intentions and constraints – because they refrained from orally discussing these parts. The aim of filling in the tsugo forms is to externalize these weakened parts. The effect of tsugo forms was remarkable in that we consequently were able to obtain the basic cards, as mentioned in Sect. 9.4, each of which included the description of the intention and constraints well as the proposed action.

9.4   Step (3): Visualize the 36 Extracted Basic Ideas and Their Correlations

After step (2), the 36 proposals with tsugo descriptions were used to obtain 36 basic cards for IMG, which is executed in this step. Then, the nuclear power plant stakeholders played the Analogy Game (AG; Chap. 5), where 20 of the 36 basic cards were randomly selected and arranged at random positions on a 2D display, each time a user played AG. The players then took operations – arranged and rearranged the cards on the basis of their intuitive interpretation of the concepts underlying the card group (see Fig. 9.10 for the this image displayed on the AG interface). When a player felt there was a concept common to a group of basic cards, s/he moved them close to each other. Thus, we assume that the co-occurrence (appearing at similar times) of a group of words in the time-series of the movement of words in AG means that some concept in the mind of the player has been hidden under those words. In this case, eight stakeholders played, creating the log of 951 operations. Thus having a dataset of 949 lines, each line including three titles (of basic cards) moved in sequential operations, we used data crystallization (DC: see Chap. 3) to visualize a map of correlations between basic cards and dummy connections among the cards. Here, a dummy connection X among cards A, B, and C suggests some latent idea relevant to A, B, and C, meaning that these three cards could possibly be combined to externalize the idea. DC visualizes this

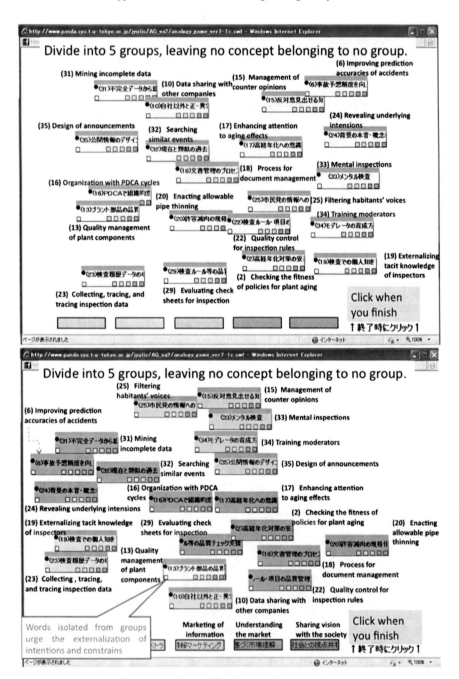

Fig. 9.10 The interface display of Analogy Game. (**a**) 20 words randomly selected from the 36 basic cards are arranged on the display. (**b**) Player rearrange these words into five groups, thinking about the contexts common to words in each group

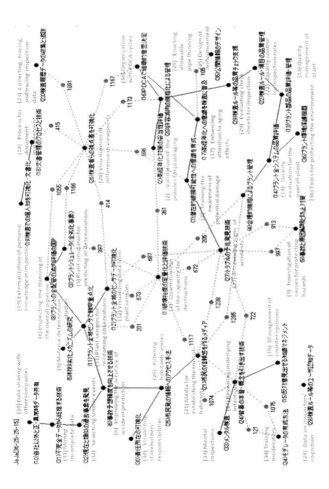

Fig. 9.11 Graph obtained by data crystallization applied to the players' AG log data for use as the IMG game board

A-B-C-X relationship with red lines connecting the A, B, and C nodes to the X node, according to the co-occurrence of events in the dataset (see Chap. 6 to review this process). This visualization is shown in Fig. 9.11. The words by the nodes are the titles of the basic cards, and each "dummy" node, such as the red one (gray in this book) denoted by an integer (e.g., "361") shows a dummy connection that implies the potential to a create an idea by combining the linked basic cards.

9.5   Steps (4) and (5): The Innovators Market Game (IMG) and Evaluations

The participants then played IMG using the graph in Fig. 9.11 as the game board (step (4)). Four inventors combined basic ideas by referring to the lines on the graph to create new ideas. They created ideas, presented them, wrote them on sticky labels, and placed them on the game board (as in Fig. 9.12). The other players are then involved in the discussion about the use scenes of the created ideas. The ideas were then revised to fit the desires/requirements of the investors and users (in this case, we did not use the word "consumers" because a new research topic on nuclear power will not be provided to end consumers). The sub-roles of the six users were the government, electric power companies, manufacturers of reactors and components, academic societies, universities, and close-proximity inhabitants, as these groups are considered to have a vested interest in the aging problem of nuclear power plants. We had no actual inhabitants who lived near a nuclear plant, so a student played this sub-role - the only exception to our preference that real stakeholders play the corresponding sub-role.

The state of the game board at the end of step (4) is shown in Fig. 9.12. After the game came the evaluation phase (step (5)), where each inventor once again presented his/her ideas and all participants evaluated the novelty, utility, and the reality on a scale of 0 (not good at all) to 5 (very good). Note that this presentation was not given by the consumers, as in previous games (see Table 6.3 in Chap. 6), but rather the inventors. The highest ranked idea in this game was
Rank (1) *"Quantitative evaluation of plant reliability by integrating a mathematical model of material deterioration and real data on the effect of aging"*, which was obtained by combining

(**11**) Plant sensors for reinforcing observations
(**21**) Plant simulator for predicting all deteriorations
(**25**) Material deterioration studies

(The numbers in parentheses above correspond to the number of the basic card.) The average evaluations by 11 referees resulted in a final score of 4.1 for novelty, 4.8 for utility, and 3.6 for reality for this idea. The other ideas and their average scores are shown in Tables 9.2 and 9.3. The results enabled us to identify the following four tendencies:

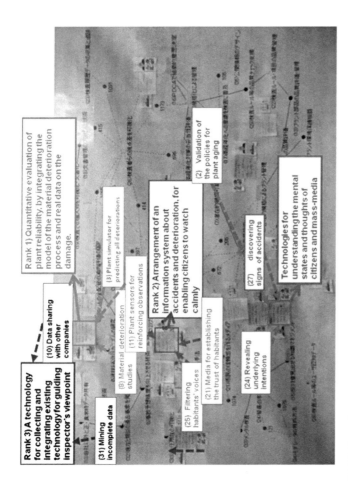

Fig. 9.12 The final state of IMG. *Dotted arrows* show how basic ideas were combined to create new ideas

Table 9.2 Ranking list of ideas and scores (1)

Demander 1	Demander 2	Demander 3	Novelty	Utility	Reality	Avr.score	Created idea	Intention	Diffused constraints	Basic cards combines
Power industry	University		4.1	4.8	3.6	4.167	Quantitative evaluation of plant reliability, by integrating the model of the material deterioration process and real data on the damage	Show the plant reliability quantitatively		3 5 11
Proposers of rules	Power industry		3.7	4.5	3.5	3.9	Arrangement of an information system about accidents and deterioration, for enabling citizens to watch calmly	Console habitants of the anxiety		12 21 25
Habitant (citizen) of the plant area			3.9	4	3.6	3.833	A technology for collecting and integrating existing technology for guiding inspector's viewpoint	Acquiring knowledge about what part the inspector should toot at		31 37
Government	Habitant	Power industry	3.8	4.2	3.5	3.833	Technologies for understanding the mental states and thoughts of citizens and mass-media	Show the evaluation of atomic plants, ny power firms, to the citizens via the government		2 24

Proposer of rules	Government	Habitant	Power industry		Rule	Goal			
	3.9	4.3	2.9	3.7	Visualize stakeholders' responsibilities, for protecting habitants from anxiety and opening the information to the public	Acquiring the truth from citizens	21	30	35
	2.9	4.2	3.8	3.633	The governmental evaluation of plant evaluation reports by the power firm and the explanation of the evaluation results	Acquiring the understanding from the nation	2	4	
	3.3	4.1	3	3.467	Knowledge management for collecting learning from, and dealing with counter opinions	Quality improvement of atomic plants	Detect seeds of troubles as early as possible	15	27

(continued)

Table 9.2 (continued)

Demander 1	Demander 2	Demander 3	Novelty	Utility	Reality	Avr.score	Created idea	Intention	Diffused constraints	Basic cards combines	
Government	Habitant	Power industry	3.3	3.2	3.8	3.433	Quality management of inspection rules, by collecting, managing, and tracing inspection data	Quality management of inspection rules		22	23
University							Studies on material deterioration, based on the revealed effects of plant quality			1 3	5 14
Proposers of rules							Create a database of (1) events in the past (2) event of other compenies and (3) the similarity relations among event features, so that the policies for protection become available for dealing with potential damages.	Training the awareness of potential damages		7 9	10 32

Table 9.3 Ranking list of ideas and scores (2)

Proposers of rules	Technologies for evaluating the effects of workers' mental state on the result of inspections and on the safety of plants		6	26	33
Habitant	Methods for designing understandable public announcement about the causes of hazards and policies for protection.	Relieving habitants	9	35	21
Proposers of rules	Technologies for extracting indivisual personal knowledge from data on utterances and actions of human	Elevating the value of documents	19	24	
Power industry	Quality management by arranging sensors for all parts of a plant, so that the damages are observed and the inspection rules becomre reinforced		11	2	28

(continued)

Table 9.3 (continued)

					14	17	28
Power industry			Solutions for enlightening workers: Environment setting for having each worker understand his/her task's contribution to lengthening the stable expectencies of a complex plant				
Government	Habitant	Power industry	A method for evaluating D ("Do") in the PDCA cycle, based on incomplete data	Improving A (action).	2	31	
Proposers of rules	Habitant	Power industry	Saving and presenting the data used for creating an explanation by the government	Enable to evaluate the responsibility of those having made the data etc, as well as the power company/ the govrnment who are generally believed to be responsible.	2	30	
University			The database of seed technologies (incl. medicine, nano-techs, etc), for realizing innovations in atomic plant technologies				

(1) The ideas with higher scores were demanded by a larger number of users.
(2) Ideas proposed by inventors who explicitly stated their intentions (among other tsugo factors) had the highest scores (all of the top eight ideas had intentions stated, whereas only four of the bottom eight did).
(3) The constraints were mostly hidden during the conversations in IMG.
(4) Unexpected similarities among players came to light. For example, there were a few similarities among those who played the power industry sub-role and those who played inhabitants (see Tables 9.2 and 9.3). Interestingly, those who played university researchers were not similar to any of the other players.

(1) may be trivial. (2) highlights the advantage of tsugology, i.e., players who have a stronger consciousness of tsugoes, especially intention, tend to create ideas that are highly evaluated. However, we should also note that we might not have considered the stakeholder constraints carefully enough. As suggested by (3), we should address an open problem for the refinement of ideas: *How can we induce participants to externalize their constraints?*

We could look at (4) from an optimistic viewpoint and assume that workers in the power industry and inhabitants who live close to power plants share an understanding about the utility of nuclear power plants thanks to their efforts to maintain communication over the decades. However, this point is controversial because the similarity among these two types of players may mean that the participants *believe*, rather than *know*, that there is a consensus between power industry workers and nearby inhabitants about the future policies of nuclear power technology. If we consider the fact that disputes and miscommunication between these two groups are a continuing problem in real society, we could take the pessimistic approach and conclude that the participants are misunderstanding the constraints of real inhabitants. This was our second motivation to solve the open problem above, which we discuss in more detail in the next section.

A note on the ideas' future value.   One year after we performed this Innovators' Marketplace process, the 2011 Tohoku Earthquake struck Japan on March 11, 2011. This earthquake, which had a magnitude of 9.0, hit the eastern half of Japan particularly hard, including the Fukushima nuclear power plants. We looked at changes in the frequencies of words on the Web that corresponded to the ideas obtained in this process and compared the frequencies with other words. Let us give an example of when we did a Google search on the top ranked ideas in Tables 9.2 and 9.3. For Table 9.4, we found that the frequency of "reliability," "deterioration," and "reliability + deterioration" had increased in the 3 months of 2011 (including March 11) as much as they had in the whole year of both 2009 and 2010, whereas other words decreased. That is, the public interest in "reliability (damaged by) deterioration" increased after we had performed the Innovators' Marketplace process. The increase for the entry "accident, information system," which corresponds to the following second-ranked idea (see Tables 9.2 and 9.3 and Fig. 9.12), was even more dramatic.

Table 9.4 The frequency of "*atomic plant, X*," where X is in the left-hand columns. The words were entered in Japanese because we were dealing with Japanese requirements and solutions relevant to nuclear plants

Word X in the query	Jan–Dec 2009	Jan–Dec 2010	Jan–March, 2011
Null	6,150,000	6,640,000	5,530,000
Aging	16,800	37,500	33,200
Deterioration	366,000	1,150,000	1,250,000
Reliability	304,000	570,000	922,000
Deterioration + reliability	28,300	65,800	69,800
Accident + information system	1,040,000	2,620,000	3,280,000

Rank (2) *Arrangement of an information system about accidents and deterioration to enable citizens to watch calmly* was obtained by combining

(11) Plant sensors for reinforcing observations
(21) Media for establishing the trust of inhabitants
(25) Filtering inhabitants' voices

According to these results, the top-ranked concepts we obtained in this process increased at a faster pace than "nuclear plant" (i.e., null in Table 9.4). We interpret these results to mean that the massive earthquake stimulated people's interest in the concepts in question more strongly than the nuclear plant itself.

9.6   Refinement, as an Extension of Step (5)

In order to solve the open problem above – "How can we induce participants to externalize their constraints?" – we distributed a questionnaire to the players to refine ideas by externalizing and reflecting the stakeholders' mutually affecting constraints. In this questionnaire, each participant was requested to write down their own tsugo (intention, and prior and posterior constraints) again. There were two differences between this task and the similar one in steps (2) and (3) . First, the participants were now able to report on the results of IMG, particularly how the ideas ranked. Second, participants had to write about both their goals and the final result, which helped them become aware of critical constraints and of the other stakeholders responsible for the constraints. They also had to write who generated their prior constraints and who would be affected by their own posterior constraints. Due to these differences, we can expect the participants to consider constraints while focusing on the ideas with the highest ranking, such as:

• Quantitatively evaluating plant reliability by integrating the model of the material deterioration process and real data on the damage.
• Arranging an information system about accidents and deterioration to enable citizens to watch calmly.

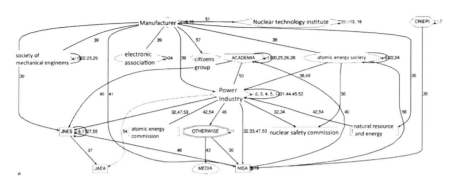

Fig. 9.13 Map of relationships among stakeholders. Each *arrow* connects players who share requirements denoted by the numbers by the *arrows* (in other words, the *arrows* show the prior and posterior constraints)

- Collecting and integrating existing technology to guide inspector's viewpoint.
- Understanding the mental states and thoughts of inhabitants.

The results of this questionnaire, which we collected from 20 participants, were visualized in a graph (Fig. 9.13) so that we could identify the requirements to/from stakeholders. The number by each arrow indicates the ID of the corresponding statement (constraint) in the list of requirements. Ten of the participants met in a room to view and discuss this graph with the aim of establishing a strategic plan. For example, the player representing the power industry considered the constraint showing that he is requested by his own staff to optimize and cement strategies to ensure security and safety, and also that manufacturers are requesting him to develop a method for hedging loss in case the power plants are shut down sooner than planned.

After discussion, all the players reached the consensus that the government should build a database that includes data related to the following:

(1) The thought processes and communications involved in making the rules, laws, and criteria for inspecting and maintaining power plants.
(2) Technical knowledge about the plant reliability and dependability, presented in a form that is readable, understandable, and useful for the average stakeholder.
(3) A Web site for frank dialogue open to all stakeholders, including experts on nuclear power plants and relevant policies as well as inhabitants.
(4) A clarification of the responsibilities of stakeholders for all kinds of accidents and affairs.

The participants came up with a plan for a master database called *"Of all people, by all people, for all people"* that includes four smaller databases storing (1) objective memories of communications and experiences, (2) scientific results of observations and experiments, (3) analytical results and communication logs, and (4) on-line communications. We want to stress again that this was the first time the participants reached a consensus throughout the entire process.

9.7 Summary

In this chapter, we presented an example of the process for externalizing essential requirements to deal with the problem of aging nuclear power plants and to ensure the safe, long-lasting use of these plants. We also demonstrated the creation of essential solutions for satisfying the requirements. The overall process is a specific application of the general Innovators' Marketplace process outlined in Chap. 8.

It is difficult to make minute improvements and to statistically validate ideas by executing many cycles the Innovators' Marketplace because stakeholders are understandably occupied by their daily work in various districts of the country. However, we can say the attention paid to intentions and constraints (from the viewpoint of tsugology) in creating and improving ideas, and the induction to both the divergence (creation/invention) and convergence of ideas via the interactive process with visualizations and reflection to further externalize tsugoes, contributed to efficiently creating and achieving a consensus with regards to a novel, useful,

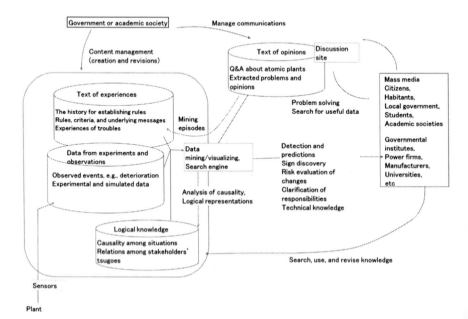

Fig. 9.14 An overview of the database "*Of all people, by all people, for all people*"

and realistic policy. Although the idea was born in a niche that was not the focus of attention for the majority, the consensus achieved was strong enough to involve all participants and influential enough to initiate a new national project.

Recently, the contribution the Innovators' Marketplace has made to power plant safety has been circulated around the atomic engineering community (Ohsawa and Nishihara 2010). For our future work, we have started a new national project to create the database shown in Fig. 9.14, which we expect to reinforce the robustness and resilience of Japan since March 11. Specifically, we aim to help Japan recover from the significant damage stemming from the Fukushima crisis caused by the earthquake and to increase tolerance against future quakes.

Reference

Ohsawa Y, Nishihara Y (2010) Innovators marketplace: process of innovative communication applied for policy marking on atomic plant aging. In: Proceedings of the international symposium on the aging management & maintenance of nuclear power plants (ISaG 2010). Mitsubishi Research Institute, Tokyo, pp 3–16

Chapter 10
IMG on the Web Versus on the Board, and Conclusion

The Innovators Market Game (IMG), as presented in the previous chapters, has been proposed as a tool for aiding innovative thought and communication. This game, which stems from our 10 years of experience with chance discovery in which data visualization is applied to the decision-making process of business teams, is able to facilitate and encourage thought and communications for innovation as well as train individuals in analogical and combinatorial thinking. In this final chapter, we compare the effect of IMG when it is used as a board game with when it is used in a Web-based environment; in other words, face-to-face application vs. Web application. We will show that there are still certain aspects of innovative communication that we can improve, some with the board game and some with the Web. Finally, we conclude this book with the proposal of a new model of cycles of interaction between inventors and consumers in the real market to show that the Innovators' Marketplace is a simplified realization of the modeled interaction.

10.1 The Outline of IMG on the Web

Although IMG was invented as a method for facilitating the process of chance discovery, we still had problems when we applied it to real business situations. The ideas created by employees of real companies who played IMG have sometimes been rejected when proposed as a business plan in their company. This problem has been partially solved by introducing the approaches reviewed in the case studies in the previous chapters. For example, we learned that some rejections were due to the violation of financial or technological (prior) constraints or (posterior) constraints due to conflict between the effects of created ideas and the current intentions of the company. We dealt with this tendency by introducing the tsugological framework and the process with multi-step cycles presented in the last two chapters. However, some problems still remained.

One, 2 h is not quite long enough for thinking, communicating, and administering the survey on relevant knowledge from external sources. Two, creating innovative

Y. Ohsawa and Y. Nishihara, *Innovators' Marketplace*, Understanding Innovation,
DOI 10.1007/978-3-642-25480-2_10, © Springer-Verlag Berlin Heidelberg 2012

ideas is difficult if participants are nervous about the playin a game, in which each idea is evaluated and criticized by other participants who might come across and serious or grave – in other words, scary. This obstacle hampers the dynamic exchange of opinions, and sometimes (although rarely) there is a silence in the middle of the game and no one says anything meaningful. Three, participants who are not gifted at oral conversation for whatever reason require a communication environment other than a meeting room. Four, positive impressions of ideas tend to weaken over time, mostly because the participants do not have any record of the utterances made during the game.

In response to these problems, we developed a Web environment in which participants can engage in a type of communication similar to that in IMG play. Participants who have played the IMG board game can later continue playing online if they like, which solves the first problem. Participants who do not like talking face-to-face or who have rusty oral communication skills can avoid these problems with the Web system, which solves the second and third problems. Finally, the communication logs are automatically recorded and available to all participants, which solves the fourth problem.

Interestingly, according to (Bargh and Mckenna 2004), the true self tends to be honestly and easily revealed in an on-line communication environment. This tendency is reflected in our daily experiences with the Web: for example, we are often brave enough to discuss about our deep or personal feelings thanks to the absence of others in front of us.

An outline of IMG on the Web (Web-IMG/Web-IM) is shown in Fig. 10.1. Each inventor creates an idea, presents it, and sticks it on the displayed game board or writes it on a bulletin board that is a list of written comments. This is where the proposed ideas will be discussed among participants. When a new idea is proposed by an inventor sticking it on the game board, the idea is automatically added to the bulletin board. Because Web-IMG players are not always in "game mode," – i.e., they tend not to pay as much attention to winning and are therefore less competitive – we sometimes call this Web-IM (Innovators' Marketplace), cutting "Game" from the name. However, in this chapter we refer to it as Web-IMG for the purpose of comparing it with IMG.

Web-IMG will have fulfilled its mission if it can facilitate innovative reasoning and communication. Web-IMG was developed with Adobe Flash Professional CS5 and uploaded to the Internet so that participants can access it from remote sites. The flow of the action is as follows.

10.1.1   Action Flow of Web-IMG

1. The player logs in to Web-IMG and views the basic cards on the game board by clicking the titles, which are shown by the graph nodes on the game board.
2. The player performs the following on his/her PC until the given time for gaming is completed.

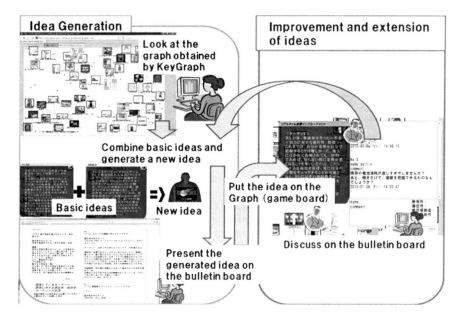

Fig. 10.1 Outline of Web-IMG (Ohsawa et al. 2010). Inventors create ideas by looking at images and basic idea cards and their relations to other ideas (*left*). The presented ideas are discussed on the bulletin board (*right*)

- Combine multiple basic cards and write any created ideas on a virtual sticky label. Created ideas also appear on the bulletin board as a leading comment that starts a new thread.

- If interested in a new idea, a player can add a comment on the bulletin board, thus progressing the discussion of that idea.

10.2 Preliminary Comparison: Board Game vs. Web Version

We compared the board game and the Web version of IMG using three conversations from each (Ohsawa et al. 2010). The evaluations below are preliminary ones that were executed only to estimate the advantages of both versions in advance. For example, if one version is superior to the other in all aspects of innovative communication, we should consider replacing our communication environment fully with the superior version. On the other hand, if one is superior in some aspects and the other in others, we should combine the two. In the following examples, 35 basic cards were created by writing summaries of existing daily-life commodities (shown in Table 10.1).

All the basic cards were used for each game in this preliminary experiment. Here, we focused on the variables corresponding to (1) metacognition, with the

Table 10.1 The 35 basic cards

(1) Anti-skid rubber	Anti-skid rubber with a 6-mm diameter, shock absorption, and noise reduction. One set has 24 pieces. Cost-effective
(2) Slippery stick	Coat the sliding lip of a door, wardrobe, or drawer to make it easier to open
(3) Smoothing pen	Pen-type lubricant for stopping scraping noise and enabling a drawer to slide more easily. Convenient to carry and use outside
(4) Seam painter	Used to clean dirty tile seams. Contains antibiotics to combat mold and dirt
(5) Concealer for furniture	Hide scratches by coating floors and wood products. Three colors in a set. Get many more colors by mixing them
(6) Target sticker for urinals	This sticker plays on men's nature to aim at a target. It prevents urine from splashing on the floor. When the stream touches the seal, the seal changes color
(7) Power mat glove	It's made of synthetic rubber, and its heat-proof temperature is 150°C! It can be used to hold the hot handle of a pan, to wrest open a jar or bottle that is difficult to turn, or to hold a pot
(8) Pushing measurement bottle	Just press it gently, and one or two spoons of the contents will be pushed out. Effective for cooking
(9) Cooking bottle	Has three thin nozzles. Put mayonnaise or ketchup inside and garnish dishes as in a restaurant
(10) Kotokoto Kun	When boiling noodles, put this in the bottom of the pot to prevent boiled-water overflow
(11) Paper carton clip	When a paper carton is opened, you can use this to clip it firmly shut. Even milk will be prevented from spilling out
(12) Microwave oven simple	Hot water can be boiled in the microwave oven. This is convenient for when you are busy
(13) Hook & bath mat clip	Use it to prevent bath mats or towels from getting wet. You can hang them to keep them clean and avoid mildew
(14) Water purifier for shower	Water purifier installed in the shower nozzle. Protects hair and skin for 2 months
(15) Sponge soap stand	Made of a coarse sponge. You can put soap on it and if it becomes dirty, simply rinse it in water
(16) Water tap lever	Enables you to open a tap when it is closed tight. A weaker person like a child or an elderly person can use it to easily turn the tap
(17) Bubble pump bottle	This bottle can make bubbles. Simply put body soap or hand soap in the bottle and shake
(18) Flex mirror	Pocket-sized mirror that can reach 50 cm when extended. You can use it to look into any kind of tight space. Try it everywhere!
(19) Screwdriver magnetizer	Screwdrivers are quickly magnetized after being rubbed with the magnetic turner. The magnetism can also be removed
(20) One-touch needle	Makes it easier to thread through the pinhole of a needle. Three kinds of needles of different lengths

(continued)

Table 10.1 (continued)

(21) Name sticker tape	Simply attach the name to a hat or sports suit with no need to iron or sew. You can freely cut it as you like
(22) Paper carton repository	Prevents carton-packed juice from splashing when squeezed it. Bottle can be left in the box before it is finished
(23) Plastic bottle hanger	Can store 2 l of liquid. It can also be turned into a watering can by attaching another pot to it
(24) Cupuled soap holder	It has a lot of suckers so that it can adhere to slippery surfaces firmly. It's also easy to peel off
(25) Glass flashing device	A cleaner for removing water and oil stains. Just scrub objects with it to flush out grime with water
(26) Ironing glove	Wear this glove on one hand and use an iron with the other. Clothes can be directly ironed when draped on a hanger
(27) Interior hook	This hook is clipped to the frame of a window. It's useful if you dislike adhesive hooks and holes in the wall
(28) Grip gem for health	Balls made of natural stone. Grip two balls in one hand to stimulate your blood circulation
(29) Remote controller wrapping film	Wrap this film around a remote controller to prevent water damage
(30) Shredder scissors	Seven razor blades quickly cut things into small pieces. It works in the kitchen as well as in the office
(31) Eye training glasses	A lot of holes are made in the glasses. When you look through the holes, your eyes are reinforced and trained
(32) Bunion pad	Relieve the pain of bunions by using this countermeasure pad. The pad can be reused
(33) Four step hair-cutter	Four types of cuts are possible. It also has a comb on it: a convenient combination
(34) Reflective strip	Put it on your bicycle or jogging shoes and you can be detected by cars up to 30 m away from you
(35) Root rot protection net	Put it at the bottom of a flower pot and the root will not rot, even if there is excess water in the saucer

externalization of one's own thoughts and senses, (2) analogical/combinatorial reasoning, and (3) context-focusing/shifting communication (see Chap. 4). The itemized descriptions below correspond to these variables and are based on the data in Table 10.2.

Deep thinking by oneself   This corresponds to metacognition, which we discussed in Chaps. 2–4. We studied six players who played both versions of IMG (board game and Web) under similar conditions. First they communicated using the IMG board game, and the next day they used Web-IMG. The time of play was fixed to 2 h for both. Strictly speaking, this is not a fair experiment because the participants might have been biased in some way due to playing the board game first. However, the results showed that five of the six players felt, after communicating in both environments, that Web-IMG was better for

Table 10.2 Comparison of board game IMG and Web-IMG

	Board game IMG			Web-IMG		
	Case 1	2	3	4	5	6
Deep thinking by oneself (%)		16.7 (1 of 6)			83.3 (5 of 6)	
Excitation(%)		66.7(4 of 6)			33.3 (2 of 6)	
Questions (%)	5.6	6.2	7.8	10.8	14.1	9.1
Negative comments	5.6	4.6	2.9	3.2	3.1	2.3
Utterance frequency	71	65	103	92	64	44
Context-shifting utterances (%)	4.98	4.72	5.82	11.82	8.65	6.55
The balance of utterance frequency (var/avr)	0.71/1.09	0.75/0.98	1.09/0.71	0.26/0.46	0.33/0.62	0.22/0.55

deep thinking by oneself without external interruptions (see Table 10.2). This negates our concern that players might have been biased by ideas presented in the board game and therefore less able to concentrate in the Web version. We thus assume that Web-IMG is a better environment for solo thinking and talking as a part of metacognition. This result is also relevant to variable (2) above (analogical/combinatorial reasoning); however, let us not yet interpret the data so extensionally.

Excitation and utterance frequency   The utterance frequency tended to be higher in the board game version than on the Web (Table 10.2). As many as four of the six participants said the board game is more exciting, which we can interpret as a sign of its suitability for metacognitive acts.

Questions   We counted the number of meaningful questions by considering their correspondence to Eris's categorization of Deep Reasoning Question (DRQ) and Generative Design Question (GDQ) (see Chap. 4), although we did not classify them into these two. These questions contributed to context-shifting (Chap. 4), but questions in general are evidence of reasoning on behalf of both inventors and consumers. As a result, questions tended to be more frequent in Web-IMG (Table 10.2). Thus, for the time being, we expect well-designed products to emerge from Web-IMG via Q&A conversations. In fact, the message-reply relations between utterances were more clearly observed in the Web-IMG communication log that that of the board game IMG.

Negative comments   Note that negative comments (such as criticisms) are not considered determents to thought and communications in IMG but rather triggers of the process to improve ideas (see Chap. 4). We counted the number of negative comments, including those from superficial expressions that were not explicitly negative as far as we could tell but that we inferred to be negative from the context. For example, the response "Wouldn't it be scary?" to the idea of a "safe lifestyle in a tunnel" is a negative impression in that it urges the presenter to reconsider the idea for improvement. The face-to-face version of IMG had a higher rate of negative comments than the Web-IMG, although the difference is not highly significant. We expect to be able to determine the hidden factors behind successful ideas by examining the negative comments in the log.

Context-shifting utterances   We counted utterances that steered the conversation toward new topics. This count was done subjectively, taking into account the reports of the six participants. As shown in Table 10.2, Web-IMG was superior in inducing this kind of utterances, and there was a significant difference between it and the board game IMG. This indicates that Web-IMG stimulates contextual shifts.

The balance of utterance frequencies   In the Web-IMG, all participants had equal opportunities to speak because there were no aggressive or super-confident individuals who might dominate the less extroverted players. As shown in Table 10.2, the variance of utterance frequency among participants was significantly less on the Web than on the board game IMG.

In summary, the board game IMG seems to be effective for enhancing excitement and drawing the attention of participants to a common area for innovation, while the Web-IMG is better for other essential features the communication agora should satisfy. In other words, Web-IMG satisfies some of the major requirements that are missing in the board game IMG. The ideal scenario is if Web-IMG is used by participants who have already played the board game version.

10.3   Comparison of the Quality and Quantity of Ideas: Board Game IMG vs. Web-IMG

Here, we restricted the basic cards to 12 (from the 35 in Table 10.3), which enabled the users to execute each game in half an hour and the authors to collect communication logs for a broad range of cases (Ohsawa and Kobashi 2011). Forty individuals participated (thirty-two men and eight women), and they were divided into ten groups (A through J) of four members. Each group held one discussion (using only board game IMG or board game and Web-IMG; discussed further below). Each group included two inventors and two consumers. The set of basic cards below were allocated to the inventors.

Each group executed the two patterns of gaming:

- (Pattern T): 30 min of board game IMG: T stands for a table game
- (Pattern T + W): 15 min of board game IMG followed by 15 min of Web-IMG

Groups A, B, C, D, and E played in pattern (T) first and then in pattern (T + W), while F, G, H, I, and J played in pattern (T + W) first and then in pattern (T). The same set of cards was used for both patterns by each group in order to ensure a fair

Table 10.3 Basic cards assigned for each group

Group	Basic cards used for the discussion
A and F	3, 9, 11, 12, 19, 20, 24, 26, 30, 21, 32, 34
B and G	7, 8, 9, 10, 11, 12, 13, 16, 22, 23, 24, 28
C and H	1, 2, 5, 6, 13, 14, 17, 18, 26, 29, 33, 35
D and I	2, 5, 6, 14, 15, 17, 19, 25, 26, 27, 33, 35
E and J	4, 6, 7, 10, 15, 20, 21, 22, 25, 26, 29, 30

comparison. Additionally, to reduce the risk of bias due to playing with the same cards, the second pattern was executed at least 1 week after the first pattern.

After both games had been completed, the participants compared the latter 15 min of each pattern, i.e., the face-to-face/on-line communication parts. Participants used a questionnaire to evaluate the patterns, ranking the following items on a scale from 0 (low) to 4 (high).

1. The utility (if the idea is convenient), reality (if it is possible to make the idea into something real with existing technologies and for a reasonable cost), and novelty of the presented idea
2. The ease of creating ideas
3. The ease of making utterances
4. The feeling of responsibility for one's own ideas
5. The quality of discussion
6. The interestingness of ideas presented

Here, we should point out that utility, reality, and novelty are not independent of each other. Results of the questionnaire showed that correlations between utility and reality and between novelty and reality were both weakly negative ($R = -0.028$ and -0.12, respectively), whereas the correlation between utility and novelty was significantly positive ($R = 0.33$). We therefore assume that the utility and novelty are approximately proportional, so here we will evaluate the quality of an idea by the product of its novelty and reality (i.e., *novelty* × *reality*).

10.3.1   The Quantity of Ideas

The number of ideas presented in the latter half of patterns (T) and (T + W) are shown in Table 10.4.

With the exception of group F, the number of ideas tended to be higher for pattern (T + W). This might sound odd if the reader recalls that, as stated in the previous section, the frequency of utterances was higher for the board game IMG. However, the frequency of sheer utterances in the preliminary experiment is essentially different from the number of ideas; that is, the numbers in Table 10.2

Table 10.4 The number of ideas

Group	Pattern (T) (board game)	Pattern (T + W) (Web)
A	5	6
B	5	6
C	3	7
D	3	6
E	4	6
F	6	3
G	4	5
H	4	5
I	4	5
J	4	5

reflect an essential feature of Web-based communication, where players tend to think on their own and then write an opinion after obtaining an idea.

With group F, which was the exception, an obtained idea about a "smoothing comb" greatly attracted participants, who sent many messages about it. The idea was to make a special comb that is chemically processed for treating hair, and the participants all asked about the scientific soundness of the product. They were all deeply focused on this discussion, so the number of presented ideas was rather low. These leads us to two conclusions: first, the introduction of Web-IMG encouraged meaningful discussion even in the exceptional case, and second, the sheer quantity of ideas is not always a good measure for evaluating the quality of a discussion environment.

10.3.2   The Ease of Communication

In terms of creating of ideas (Fig. 10.2), we found that using both the board game and the Web version made it easier to create ideas than using just the board game. This points to the influence of *deep thought by oneself*, as presented in the preliminary experiment.

In addition, making utterances is easier with the Web than with the board game, as shown in Fig. 10.3. In a superficial sense, this contradicts the results of Table 10.2, which shows that the utterance frequency with the Web is lower than with the board game. However, participants tended to feel that the "ease of making utterances" was equivalent to the number of meaningful comments rather than the sheer frequency of utterances including snippets such as "Yeah!," "Hmmm," "Nice!," etc. That is, participants on the Web tended to focus more on the presentation of a new idea and comments for improving this idea. In this sense, we should regard the ease of making utterances as the ease of making meaningful comments about ideas. As with focusing on the number of created ideas rather than the frequency of utterances, we consider this result a reflection of solo thinking while working with a PC at one's

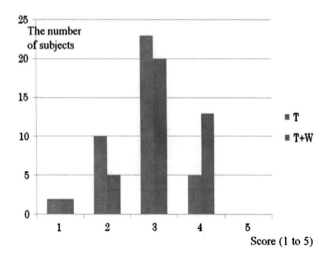

Fig. 10.2 The ease of creating ideas

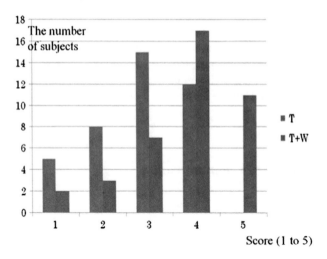

Fig. 10.3 The ease of making utterances

own desk. With these results, there was no significant difference between groups A, B, C, D, and E and groups F, G, H, I, and J.

10.3.3   The Quality of Ideas

In terms of achieving innovation, the quality of ideas is more important than the quantity because innovation does not mean the sheer generation of ideas but rather the creation of ideas that will be accepted by a market and make a strong impact

Table 10.5 Comparison of the quality of ideas

	Average quality of ideas	
	Board game	Web
A	4	3.5
B	8.2	3.833
C	8.333	3.714
D	9.333	3.833
E	5.5	8
F	4.667	5
G	3	5.8
H	3.5	9.6
I	9.5	7.8
J	9	7

while doing so. In this respect, we re-evaluated the quality we defined previously (the product of novelty and reality). The results are shown in Table 10.5. We evaluated ideas number 42 and 54 for the latter halves of pattern (T) (board game) and pattern (T + W) (Web).

There is no significant difference between the left and the right columns (the board game and the Web), and there was no significant difference between groups A, B, C, D, and E and groups F, G, H, I, and J. This means we do not have to consider any differences due to the order of patterns (T) and (T + W).

A tentative conclusion from these results may be that pattern (T + W) is superior to pattern (T), because the former makes everything easier (the creation of ideas and the utterance of meaningful comments) and enables participants to obtain ideas of an equal quality as pattern (T). However, we draw your attention to the following result in Fig. 10.4, which is significant in terms of real communication for innovation. As you can see in the figure, the board game players felt more responsible for the ideas they had created than the Web players did. This result, combined with the result shown in Table 10.2, can be interpreted as meaning that an environment in which the created ideas may be criticized by others makes each participant extremely careful about making their presentations – and also about evaluating the presentations of others. Although the context-shifting comments in the Web-IMG are more frequent than in the board game (Table 10.2), which is expected to encourage free discussions without constraints, this freedom from constraints means the participants are relaxing too much and not taking enough responsibility for their own ideas and comments. This reminds us of Finke's experiments, which we described in Chap. 4: some constraints on basic knowledge and on the resultant ideas accelerates the creation of useful ideas, as demonstrated by the cases in Chap. 5, where players of the Analogy Game (AG) externalized concepts when they got trapped in a dead-lock state due to assigned constraints.

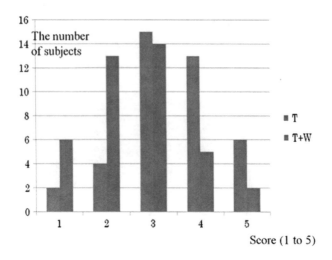

Fig. 10.4 The feeling of responsibility for one's own ideas

10.4   The Comparison of Communication Qualities

Here, we classify utterances into four categories:

(a) Utterances by inventors presenting their ideas
(b) Responses to utterances in (a)
(c) Utterances for improving an idea's value (by inventors or consumers: No investors in this case)
(d) Others

The number of utterances in each category is shown in Table 10.6, on which we can obtain the ratio of category (c) over all the utterances in each case, as in Fig. 10.5.

The difference between patterns (T + W) and (T) – that the value improvements are more frequent in the former than in the latter – is obviously significant. For example, let us look at a part of the case of (T + W) for group F, where the best idea (utility: 2, reality: 3, novelty: 3) was created by combining the two basic cards below from Table 10.1. The utterances denoted by (c) are of category (c).

(24) **Cupuled soap holder**   It has a lot of suckers so that it can adhere to slippery surfaces firmly. It's also easy to peel off.
(26) **Ironing glove**   Wear this glove on one hand and use an iron with the other. Clothes can be directly ironed when draped on a hanger.

I propose a mitten with cupules. (An idea combining (24) and (26).)
How is it different from an ordinary mitten? (c)
Does anyone know why the mitten does not have five fingers? Is it to make
it easier to carry heavy baggage?

Table 10.6 The number of utterances in categories (a), (b), (c), and (d)

	Latter half of pattern (T)				Latter half of pattern (T + W)			
	(a)	(b)	(c)	(d)	(a)	(b)	(c)	(d)
A	5	1	0	1	6	5	2	0
B	5	0	1	0	6	0	3	0
C	3	0	0	0	7	1	4	1
D	3	1	1	0	6	2	3	0
E	4	0	0	0	6	3	1	1
F	6	1	0	0	3	2	5	2
G	4	1	1	2	5	1	4	2
H	4	3	1	0	5	2	2	1
I	4	3	0	2	5	2	4	3
J	4	1	1	1	5	5	3	3

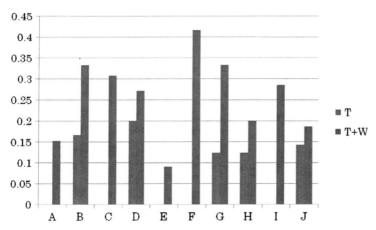

Fig. 10.5 The ratio of category (c) over utterance in each case

The mitten has cupules so that objects with a smooth surface can be carried without slippage.

Maybe we need a different material to ensure proper sanitation. Why don't you propose a cover in the lid handle of a pot? (Another idea combining (24) and (26).) (c)

It looks difficult to use.

I already have one like that, but it gets dirty very easily. Annoying... It needs improvements. (c)

By the way, I propose scissors for cutting a fine curve regardless of the angle. (An idea combining (20) and (30) below.)

The last line is presenting a new idea, obtained by combining the two basic cards below, that scored 3 for utility, 1 for reality, and 3 for novelty. In actual fact, the idea cannot be directly derived by combining these two cards. We should point out meaningful questions of "how" i.e., of the GDQ and "why" i.e., of the DRQ types of Eris (see Chap. 4) work in improving ideas, and sometimes urge participants to give up hopeless ideas and also to shift the context. These known effects correspond with the results of the preliminary test in Table 10.2.

(20) **One-touch needle**   Makes it easier to thread through the pinhole of a needle. Three kinds of needles of different lengths.

(30) **Shredder scissors**   Seven razor blades quickly cut things into small pieces. It works in the kitchen as well as in the office.

Here is another example from the same Web-IMG game:

Let me propose a furniture cleaner by combining (5) and (25).
You may be able to hide the scratch, but it is not an essential treatment.
    I think this combination might be able to do it. (c)
By combining (2) and (33), I propose a smoothing comb.
    Its surface is chemically processed so that the hair will be smoothed
    when combed.
This already exists, doesn't it? How is it structured?
Maybe the surface is very smooth...?
A rinse treatment comb would be more convenient.
    (Improvement of the idea.) (c)
A hot comb that absorbs liquid? That might be too complex,
    because you'd have to isolate the thermal metamorphism of a protein. (c)

The four basic cards used here are as follows.

(2) **Slippery stick**   Coat the sliding lip of a door, wardrobe, or drawer to make it easier to open.

(5) **Concealer for furniture**   Hide scratches by coating floors and wood products. Three colors in a set. Get many more colors by mixing them.

(25) **Glass flashing device**   A cleaner for removing water and oil stains. Just scrub objects with it to flush out grime with water.

(33) **Four step hair-cutter**   Four types of cuts are possible. It also has a comb on it: a convenient combination.

The basic cards used are changed extensively during play, similarly to the previous example, although the context is partially maintained, i.e., the context is still the treatment of damaged things (hair and furniture). We can see, in both examples, that the components for creating ideas and the methods for realizing an intention can be easily shifted due to the environment of online remote communication where participants do not have to consider each other's emotions, which is quite significant in terms of creating new ideas. This shift was rarely seen in pattern (T) cases, where the only communication was face-to-face as participants played the board game. Such shifts sometimes discourage participants from reaching their goal of creating a product or service that is satisfactory for all participants, as seen in both examples.

Table 10.7 The number and quality of proposed ideas in three categories

	Utterance category	No. of proposed ideas	Average quality of ideas
Latter half (15 min) of pattern (T)	a	42	6.286
	b	0	–
	c	0	–
Latter half (15 min) of pattern (T + W)	a	40	6.05
	b	6	5.167
	c	8	4

Let us discuss the relationship between the quality of ideas and situations in which the utterances proposing the ideas were made. Here, we categorize the situations as (a), (b), or (c), corresponding to the (a), (b), and (c) utterances we mentioned above. That is,

(a) The idea was uttered by an inventor as he or she presented it.
(b) The idea was uttered as a response to an utterance type (a).
(c) The idea was born after improving an idea's value (by either inventors or consumers).

As in Table 10.7, the number of ideas in each of these categories is shown, with the average of quality (defined by the product of novelty and reality) of the ideas. We find ideas tend strongly to be presented by the inventors rather than by consumers as informal suggestions, in the IMG on the board. On the other hand, the ideas can be proposed by consumers informally in the case of Web-IMG. These results may be interpreted superficially that the Web-based communication worked for easily improving the ideas with reflecting consumers' opinions.

However, we cannot accept this superficial interpretation if we look at the rightmost column of Table 10.7. According to the average quality of ideas in Table 10.7, the ideas presented by inventors are of higher quality than the others ($p < 0.05$). Especially in the cases of pattern (T), the inventors' ideas are of higher quality than ideas inserted by consumers. That is, the fruits of communications are reflected to inventors' proposals, implicitly in the case of board game, whereas the fruit appears by real time in the bulletin board on the Web. Participants may often feel the quality of communication is higher on the Web than on the board, but the indirect effect of ripening the fruits in the IMG on the board, which is difficult to feel for participants, is meaningful for accomplishing a useful, realistic, and novel ideas.

10.5 Summary

It is natural in the evolution of technological development to replace humans with automated systems such as cars, robots, computers, etc. In this sense, we expect that using IMG on the Web, where the face-to-face communication of the IMG board game is moved to an online computer system, will overcome some of the drawbacks of the board game version. For example, time constraints and problems related to personality type (reluctance to speak in a group, to listen to others, etc.) can be reduced by using computer technology. In addition, communication logs are easier to store if everything takes place online. The benefits of an online communication environment are self-evident.

However, when the gaming conditions (communication time, preset basic cards) were the same, we found that neither approach was superior to the other in terms of the quality of ideas created, in spite of the fact that it is easier to communicate and to contribute value-improving utterances on the Web. Our experimental results showed that the sense of responsibility players felt for their own ideas when playing the board game version was the key element that kept it on par with the Web version. This sense of responsibility is just as essential as the questions and criticisms we mentioned in Chap. 4 in terms of obtaining high-quality ideas because it means that players are more careful about their own intentions and constraints as well as those of others, including consumers, although granted this might make some utterances more difficult.

10.6   Some Concluding Observations

Based on the results above, let us present the final conclusion of the book. Constraints and intentions – called tsugoes in this book – are often ignored in dialogues among inventors, among consumers, and between inventors and consumers. This occurs more often in dialogues between inventors and investors, because these two parties rarely communicate with each other.

We can explore this loss of information by focusing on the two sides, inventors and consumers, who communicate with each other relatively often. In Fig. 10.6, two cycles, called the I-cycle and the C-cycle, are bridged via communications between I (inventors) and C (consumers). The inventors propose a product/service, develop it, and launch it in the market, and the analysis of its performance is and tacit experiences acquired in the market shall be fed back to the development of new proposals, as in the cycle of A $\rightarrow$ B $\rightarrow$ C $\rightarrow$ K $\rightarrow$ A (the I-cycle). The consumers interact with the product/service (buy it or borrow it, etc.), evaluate it, discuss their experiences with other consumers and with providers (including inventors), and refer back to these communications and experiences in their interactions with future products or services, as in the cycle of E $\rightarrow$ F $\rightarrow$ G $\rightarrow$ H $\rightarrow$ F (the C-cycle).

Two additional cycles in the market and in the various communication environments form a bridge between the I- and C-cycles:

- The cycle of product dealing. Advertise, sell, and collect the data on the real behaviors of customers and products/services. Advertisements have recently been seen as a kind of communication, but here we mean the one-way

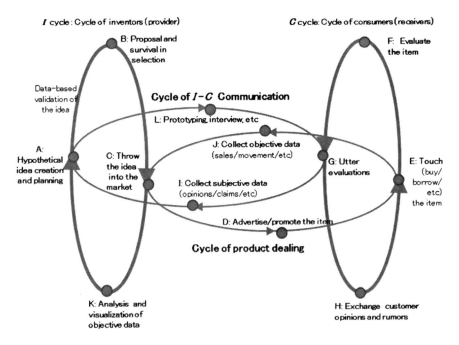

Fig. 10.6 The four-cycle model of innovator interactions in the marketplace

presentation on behalf of inventors of things they want to sell. This is shown as the path of D → E → F → G → I in this chart.

- The cycle of I–C communication. Consumers who evaluated the product/service at point G, or the idea proposed at point L before selling, send messages to the inventor side. These messages are considered data by the inventor at point I. Methods for requirement acquisition such as the one presented by Carrol (2000) and innovating thinking methods as systematized in (Plattner et al. 2010) are in this cycle, as well as the designers' individual thoughts. These contributions have points in common with methods for marketing, such as consumer interview methods (Vaughn et al. 1996), also dedicated to I–C communication.

We should note that a bit of information drops away in each of these cycles. For example, the constraints and intentions of the consumers when they use daily commodities such as proposed in the cases in this chapter, are not completely discussed at points G or I because the time and situation are different from point F. In such cases, participants should make sure to take responsibility for the created ideas – that is, to consider the constraints and intentions of stakeholders as thoroughly as possible – in order to create really useful items. In other words, the more responsible participants feel, the better the obtained ideas are to be obtained, especially in the case of daily commodities (we cannot always declare this for other kinds of products). This is why the board game version of IMG outperforms Web-IMG in the quality of ideas, in spite of Web-IMG's superiority in other aspects.

Our overall approach is to approximately model communications for innovation (as in Fig. 10.6) and estimate the effect of communications on the realization of innovation. The Innovators' Marketplace is a process consisting of two sides – inventors and consumers – who are all innovators and interacting with each other in order to communicate about products and services. In this book our main focus has been conceptual communications, but we also place importance on the cycles of product movement and I–C communication. Step (5) of the Innovators' Marketplace process (see Chap. 8) is meant to be customized to the purpose of the players: while it can be used to evaluate proposed ideas and monitor the extent of conflicts as a feedback to following cycles in the process (Chap. 8), it can also be used to refine ideas by considering real social constraints (Chap. 9). In cases where daily commodities are being dealt with (as in the examples in this chapter), step (5) can be used to test prototypes of the proposed products or even the real products themselves. If players want to test a product in the real market, we conduct step (5) to collect a sufficient amount of sale data and/or questionnaires asking consumers of the product to rate their satisfaction. It is also possible to test a product using step (4), provided it is a simple one like the one in Fig. 10.7 (the created product here is a colander for washing clothes). Such testing of real products is a crucial step in the creation of realistic, high-quality products, as has been pointed out in other recent studies (Plattner et al. 2010).

In closing, we recommend readers take the process of the Innovators' Marketplace we have described in this book and customize it to their unique style of activities. However, if this feels too difficult, just remember to enjoy the game: the cycle continues no matter where you start, and the important thing is to remember how interesting and enjoyable it can be.

Fig. 10.7 Transforming an idea into a real object by combining the commodities

References

Bargh JA, Mckenna KYA (2004) The internet and social life. Annu Rev Psychol 55:573–590

Carrol JM (2000) Making use: scenario-based design of human-computer interactions. MIT press, Cambridge

Ohsawa Y, Okamoto K, Takahashi Y, Nishihara Y (2010) Innovators marketplace as game on the table versus board on the Web. In: Proceedings of the ICDM Workshops, pp 816–821, University of Technology, Sydney, December 2010

Ohsawa, Y., and Kobashi, R., Comparison of Design Communications on the Table versus on the Web for Daily Commodities - Validating a Model of Provider-Recipient Interaction, Japan Marketing Journal Vol.32 No.2, 2011, pp.19–33 (in Japanese)

Plattner H, Meinel C, Leifer L (2010) Design thinking: understand-improve-apply. Springer, Berlin/Heidelberg

Vaughn S, Schumm JS, Sinagub JM (1996) Focus group interviews in education and psychology. Sage, Thousand Oaks/London

Index